BLIND OBEDIENCE

BLIND OBEDIENCE

A True Story of Family Loyalty and Murder in South Georgia

Bill Boyd

Mercer University Press
2000

ISBN 0-86554-707-6
MUP/H525

© 2000 Mercer University Press
6316 Peake Road
Macon, Georgia 31210-3960

First Edition.

∞The paper used in this publication meets the minimum requirements of American National Standard for Information Sciences—Permanence of Paper for Printed Library Materials, ANSI Z39.48-1984.

Library of Congress Cataloging-in-Publication Data

CIP data are available from the Library of Congress

Contents

To Mildred Rawlins Burch,
Whose curiosity is the foundation of this book,

and
Albert S. Pendleton, Jr.
Whose curiosity added priceless color to this story

ACKNOWLEDGMENTS

BECAUSE THIS BOOK IS BASED ON HAPPENINGS ALMOST A century ago, material was gathered from many sources to reconstruct these events. Here is a list of people—not complete, I'm sure, but certainly intended to be—who contributed invaluable time and effort:

Mildred Rawlins Burch told her husband that she grew to adulthood, married, and moved away from home before she learned that her grandfather, Joe Rawlins, had been hanged for murder. She said her children and grandchildren would not have to wonder. So she gathered information with the idea of writing a book before her unexpected death in 1984. Without her research and interviews in the 1950s, 1960s and 1970s, this book probably would never have been written.

Albert S. Pendleton, patriarch of the Lowndes County Historical Society, wrote a college paper on the case in 1971 and interviewed a number of people with direct knowledge of the trials and the aftermath. He generously shared his notes and thoughts on the case.

Members of all three principal families—the Carters, the Rawlinses, and the Jowerses—were cooperative and helpful. My special thanks to Clarice Roberts and Janice Roquemore, great-granddaughters of W.L. Carter; Brenda Sharpless, Janice Coatney, and John H. Rawlins Jr., great-grandchildren of Joe Rawlins; Philip Jowers and Kim Jowers Gilliard, descendants of J.J. "Squire" Jowers. My gratitude also to Harvey Burch for relating many additional stories that were not included in the book by his late wife, Mildred.

Thanks also to the dozens of people who helped with my research and photographic efforts, including Sara L. Crow, Lowndes County Clerk of Superior Court; Andy Phrydas, a records analyst at the Georgia Department of Archives and History; Alan Morgan, curator for the Lowndes County librarians at the *Macon Telegraph*; and the Washington Memorial Library.

Last, but certainly not least, my thanks to the best team of editors and proofreaders any author could ever want—Barbara Stinson, Bill Weaver, Marc Jolley, and Bill Thompson.

PROLOGUE

NO ONE SEEMS QUITE SURE HOW THE FEUD BETWEEN JOSEPH G. Rawlins and William L. Carter began. Rawlins' descendants today say it took root in the 1870s in Telfair County where Rawlins grew up. Carter's descendants say they didn't know if Carter—who frequently bought and sold property and moved often from place to place—ever lived in Telfair County.

Rawlins' descendants believe that Carter pursued Rawlins for some unexplained reason and twice bought land next to him, first in Coffee County and again in Lowndes County, after having difficulties in Telfair County. Carter told a neighbor that it was just a weird coincidence that he twice bought land bordering Rawlins' land in two locations fifty-five miles apart.

Regardless of what started the feud, it proved to be an enduring one, spanning as many as twenty-seven years. And it pitted two men who were gifted—perhaps tragically—with the grit to stand up to other people.

Joe Rawlins' moods and actions swung from one extreme to the other. He was a boy dedicated to caring for his mother and sisters, and a wayward teen-ager who lived and fought too much like a man. He was a devout Christian and preacher on one hand and on the other hand, an intensely jealous husband whose temper seemed to know no bounds when he was riled. He could be a caring friend or a dangerous enemy.

W. L. Carter, on the other hand, read law books and often took people to court. Even though he seemed to keep to himself most of the time, he had a knack for making far too many enemies.

Even though the two men battled both physically and emotionally in the fields, on the roads, and in the courts, it's doubtful they knew how much they had in common.

Both grew up without the influence of a father through their most impressionable years. Rawlins' father deserted the family when Joe was thirteen. Carter's father died of Civil War injuries when Carter was fourteen.

Both were forced to become men in their early teens, and those early years forged a tough, never-back-down demeanor in both men.

Both were family men who cherished their children. Carter fathered nine children, Rawlins five.

Both were ordained ministers, Rawlins in the Baptist faith and Carter as a Methodist. Both backed away from preaching. Rawlins gave it up after he moved away from Coffee County, and Carter lost his license because of inactivity.

What sustained the feud is as uncertain as what started it. But several points seem clear. First, while the feud only simmered at times, it didn't end until Joe Rawlins and a hired hand, Alf Moore, were hanged in 1905. Second, efforts by mutual acquaintances could never bring peace between the two men. Third, they never met face to face in any mindset except acrimony.

While this case found its place in Georgia history as one of the most infamous murders of all time, history may have been made in several other areas. First, the clamor for information about the case turned the *Valdosta Times* into a daily newspaper. Second, the testimony of Moore, who joined the nighttime raid in which two Carter children were killed, was the key to Joe Rawlins' conviction. And it may have been the first time in Georgia history that the testimony of a black man put a white man on the gallows. Third, Macon attorney John Randolph Cooper, who defended Rawlins and his sons, may have started the trend toward lengthy appeals. In a time—the early part of the twentieth century—when even death sentences were usually carried out within a couple of months after the trial ended, Cooper took the Rawlins case to the Georgia Supreme Court twice and the U.S. Supreme Court twice. He delayed the hangings for sixteen months after the verdict, which might have been a record at the time. Less than ten years later, the criminal backlog became so great that the Georgia Court of Appeals was created.

This book is based on:

- Extensive research that includes more than four hundred pages of court transcripts and about one hundred and sixty newspaper clippings.
- A book written by Mildred Rawlins Burch, a granddaughter of Joe Rawlins.
- A college thesis written in 1971 by Albert S. Pendleton of Valdosta and other notes he accumulated when witnesses to the trial were still alive.
- Interviews with dozens of people, including members of all three principal families — the Carters, the Rawlinses and the Jowerses.

The author has taken some liberties in recreating the earlier events in this book, some of which are based on hand-me-down stories through three or four generations. But most of it is derived from court records, trial transcripts, and newspaper accounts.

Joe Rawlins and his family. L–R: Milton, Leonard, Jessie, Joe, a
daugther, Angeline holding second daughter, unknown.

Squire and Rachel Jowers, parents of Angeline Rawlins.

J. G. Rawlins

Milton Rawlins

Leonard Rawlins

Jessie Rawlings

A photograph of the courthouse toady where the trials took place.

Inside the courthouse today.

John Randolph Cooper, defense attorney for the Rawlins's.

W. E. Thomas, Lowndes County
Solicitor.

The tombstone of Joe Rawlins with the infamous epitaph:

This bark was well built but misguided,
Run swift on the rocks of destruction.

South Georgia 1905

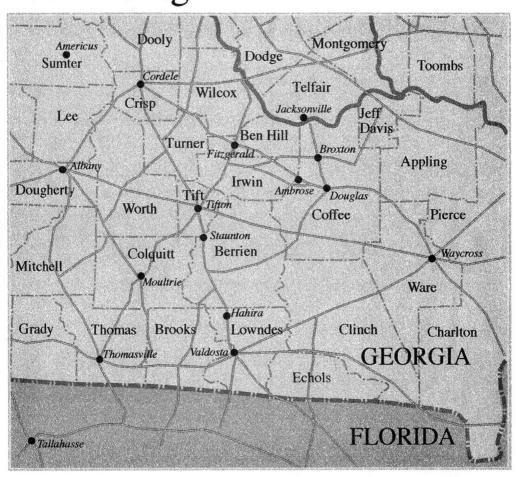

1

JOE RAWLINS STOOD ON THE PORCH OF THE LOG CABIN HIS father had built two years before he was born and watched the setting sun. His mind was occupied not by the beauty of what he saw, but an uncertain future. During his usual two-mile walk home from school that day and during another hour of chores around the family's farm, his mind had been occupied by thoughts far more serious than most boys not yet fourteen might have to consider. And he'd arrived at a decision that he knew would change his life.

As the last rays of sunlight warmed his face on that late-February evening, he knew he would quit school to plow the fields. There was no one else to do it. His father was gone. Again. He left when the crops were in the fields last year, and Joe had a feeling—an awful, sinking feeling deep in the pit of his stomach—that his father would not return this time.

The squeak of the front door hinges told him that his mother had come outside. She took a seat on a settee behind him. Joe knew it was his mother and not one of his sisters, even though he didn't turn around. The smell of fresh-baked bread or pies seemed to cling to her, and he loved that aroma. No one could bake better cakes and pies and cookies than Polly Ann Rawlins, and a large slice of strawberry pie had reminded him of that a few minutes earlier.

Even though Joe might normally have complimented her on the pie, Polly noticed that her son was silent and engrossed in deep thought.

"What's on your mind, Joey?" she asked.

Joe disliked that name. It made him sound like a baby. He was almost six feet tall, and he wished she would call him just plain Joe. But his mother always had called him Joey, and she probably always would.

"It's about Pa," Joe said, turning to face his mother. "Plowin' shoulda started a couple of weeks ago, and it ain't gettin' done."

"Well, I'm looking for some hired help," his mother said.

"Ma, we cain't afford no hired help, and you know it," he said. "We didn't do very good last year, and I know money's tight. We'll have to sell some livestock to buy seed for this year. You told me that."

"I know, Joey, but … Well, don't worry, we'll just have to work it out."

"Ain't but one thing to do, Ma. I've gotta quit school and do the work myself."

"No, Joey."

"Yes, Ma. It's the only way. You really don't think Pa is comin' back, do you?"

He waited for an answer. After a long pause, he stepped closer to his mother. "Tell me the truth, Ma. You don't really think Pa is comin' back this time, do you? He's been gone almost a year, and this time, he's gone for good, ain't he?"

As Joe stood there, dreading the truth but knowing in his heart what it was, he saw tears well up in his mother's eyes. As the first one ran down his mother's cheek, it glistened like a diamond in the glow of the sunset. Joe hoped that his sisters would not come outside right then. He needed an answer, an honest answer, from his mother about the situation.

So he sat down next to her on the settee his father had built from willow a dozen years ago. Her hands reached out and held his.

"Joey, you're such a smart boy," she said. "I wanted you to go to school some day in McRae and get a real good education."

"It's OK, Ma, I know my numbers. I can trade with folks and not get cheated. Remember how I hauled the corn and peas to town last summer? I did all right, didn't I?"

"Of course, you did."

"Well, I can read and write pretty good. I can handle things on the farm, too."

"I know, but I wanted…" Her voice trailed off.

"I know, Ma. All of us—you, me, the girls—we all wanted somethin' better. But you've said yourself that we've gotta do what we've gotta do to make a livin'. And I've gotta do the plowin'. Startin' tomorrow…."

Polly Ann sat there holding her son's hands, gazing at him in wonderment. How did he understand this emptiness that James Rawlins had left behind? Her husband had deserted his family just like his own father had once deserted him. Did this sort of behavior run in the family? She shuddered at the thought.

One thing for certain, she was thinking, a boy as young as her Joey should not have to deal with running a farm. Most boys at thirteen wouldn't think of doing what he'd just suggested. Most simply would not be mature enough to shoulder such responsibility. But her Joey?

She reached over and held him close. She was very lucky to have a hard-working boy, especially since he was her only son.

Martha, the oldest of Joe's sisters, called from inside the house, and Joe went to help with her school work. Polly Ann stayed on the porch and her thoughts wandered back….

Had it really been fifteen years since they'd married and built this log cabin? Even though Reconstruction was under way in the South at the time and there never seemed to be enough money, she and James worked side by side, adding rooms onto the house as more children arrived and clearing more land for crops.

For ten years, they had worked hard and built up their holdings. The farm grew from just over thirty acres to almost a hundred. Cows, chickens, guineas, goats and hogs thrived on their land, and the Rawlinses prospered. But when James began taking extended "hunting" trips the past couple of years, she'd been forced to sell off some of the livestock to make ends meet. And now her only son was going to quit school and do the work of a man—the work his father ought to be doing.

Shaking her head at the demise of her marriage, she wondered if she'd done something to deserve such a fate. No woman wanted to be alone. No one wanted to be a deserted wife. People whispered about women whose husbands left them. Was there something wrong with that woman? Was she not a good wife? Or a good mother? Or a good lover?

Polly Ann truly had loved James when they'd married in 1864. She'd loved him even more when each of their four children were born—first Joey in 1865, then Martha, Priscilla Ann, and finally, Mary.

It had seemed like the perfect family with the eldest a boy who was so much like his father and then three girls who were bright and pretty and healthy. She treasured the memories of dressing up her babies to go to services each Sunday at Blockhouse Church. And she relished her role as a wife and mother. She did not want to have to be a father, too, and have to run the farm.

But James just wouldn't settle down. Folks who attended Blockhouse Church had warned her that a wild streak ran through James Rawlins. However, she had believed that if she could feed him well enough, love him passionately enough and praise him often enough, everything would be all right. But it wasn't.

Polly Ann knew from the outset that James was a dedicated hunter and trapper, and she liked that. In the lean years when they were first married, he brought home meat to be cured and pelts to be traded for staples they did not grow on the farm. Not only did his forays along the Ocmulgee River assure her that they would never go hungry, but James produced a nice extra income with the furs.

For ten years, James diligently worked the land and confined his hunting trips to the off-season. But recently, the trips lengthened from a few days into a month or more. On one occasion, he disappeared for more than two months. When Polly Ann went into Jacksonville on the weekend, she heard talk that James had been seen there and that he was, as one person told her, "messin' with other women."

When James finally returned, he brought few furs and he seemed cold to her thoughts of affection. Then he began taking hunting trips during the growing season, and Polly Ann was forced to work long hours in the fields to try to keep the crops in good shape. During his father's absences, her Joey also worked harder than ever. With his help, Polly Ann harvested the crops, too.

James was at home once just long enough for Polly Ann to get pregnant with their fourth child, and then he disappeared for more than a year. The struggle to keep things going overwhelmed Polly Ann, but she managed to hang on, hoping every minute of every day that her husband would come back before the baby was born.

He didn't. Polly Ann sent her Joey to get a midwife to deliver Mary.

Polly Ann's worries were soon etched into her face. When she looked in the mirror, she could see lines that a woman barely thirty years old should not have. And, more and more often, her Joey was required to be the man of the house.

After being gone for a year, James showed up one day in the fall of 1876 and tried to act like he'd never been away. Joe, still a trusting child at age eleven, obviously wanted to put his father's long absence in the past. They hunted and fished together, and a bond began to develop. His father would slap him on the back when he caught a large fish or made a kill and say, "You're just a chip off the old block, son." And Joe's chest would swell with pride.

However, Martha, eldest of the three girls, never did warm up to her father. She'd just turned ten, and she understood her mother's front-porch vigil and why she sometimes couldn't hold back the tears. James was going to have to do more than just pat her on the back if he was going to claim Martha's affection.

But, as suddenly as James had returned, he rode away from the log cabin early one morning in December 1878, stopped at a cousin's house in Jacksonville to eat and then disappeared for good.

As the truth became apparent to Joe, his bitterness toward his father grew, and he freely voiced those feelings any time his father's name was mentioned. The birth of Mary had been especially scary for Joe, and he knew he would never forgive his father's absence at such an important time.

The hurt ran deep inside Joe, and he soon realized that he could never trust his father again. James Rawlins' final exit motivated Joe to do something his mother would never forget. He knelt at Polly Ann's knee one evening and said, "Ma, I won't never leave you and the girls like Pa did. I'll take care of y'all. I promise."

His mother started crying. Some of the tears were shed for the sad truth of the situation, but most were tears of happiness that she had a son with a good heart and good intentions. She held his hands until Joe became uncomfortable with the tears. Then he got up and went to his room.

There, he cried, too.

Polly Ann shook off the memories and thought about the present. Maybe Joey couldn't handle it. Maybe she would have to go ahead with a plan that had been forming in her mind over the past few months. She really ought to find someone to farm her acreage on the halves. Then she could move the children to town so they'd be closer to school and Joey wouldn't have to become a man before his time.

Spring planting kept Joe too busy to think about school and the friends he'd left behind. For more than a year he never went near the school while it was in session. He didn't want to have to explain that he'd quit school because his father had deserted the family. But he would see his friends in Jacksonville, a rough-and-tumble town near the ferry that crossed the Ocmulgee River on the road between McRae and Douglas.

On one occasion, he ran into his teacher. She complimented him on the decision he made about farming but said she hoped he might return to school one day. She also told him how each of his classmates was doing. He smiled at each bit of news.

But the trip had a drawback, too. Joe saw W. L. Carter on the streets of Jacksonville. Carter was another problem left behind by Joe's father. Animosity between James Rawlins and Carter had arisen during James' last year at home. Carter had accused James Rawlins of stealing some hogs. But an investigation by the sheriff revealed that Carter had sold the hogs to a man across the river in Coffee County.

Joe never knew why the two men feuded, but he inherited the situation and he wasn't going to back away from it.

The hog-stealing incident branded Carter as a liar, and he didn't take it lightly. He sought vengeance against Joe, making snide or cutting remarks whenever he saw young Rawlins. He said something to Joe that day in Jacksonville.

Joe did not like the man, and the feeling was mutual. Joe considered a round of fisticuffs that day, even though he was a dozen years younger than Carter, but he decided to let it pass.

When he arrived at home late in the afternoon, he told his mother about the meeting with Carter. "Someday," he said, "I'm going to kick his ass."

His mother admonished him for his language and told him to forget Carter. "He's a troublemaker," Polly Ann said. "Just leave him be. He's not worth the bother."

Apparently, no one realized how deep Joe's feelings ran toward Carter, perhaps not even Carter himself. But he kept his word about what he'd told his mother. A couple of years later, the two men met again in downtown Jacksonville. Joe had packed two years worth of ropy muscles on his slender frame working in the fields, and he was a man-sized boy at age fifteen.

Sure enough, Carter saw Joe and announced to several men in front of the general store, "There's that thievin' Rawlins kid who was too dumb to finish school."

By the time the last word was uttered, a stinging right landed on Carter's jaw, and the fight was on. A crowd gathered as the combatants rolled around on the ground, hitting, scratching, and kicking. Finally, the town marshal fired a shot in the air to break up the gathering and stop the scuffle.

When Joe arrived home that afternoon, he wanted to wash up at the well before his mother saw him, but Polly Ann was working outside.

"What happened?" she asked.

"I whupped Carter's ass," Joe said. That might have been an overstatement since both sustained cut lips and bruised cheekbones, but Joe obviously was happy with the result because he figured he'd taken on the town bully and won at least a partial victory.

Polly Ann bit her lip. She started to admonish her son for his language. But then she thought about the past two years. With help from Polly Ann's brothers, Joe had grown and harvested two crops, and they were good crops, too. He was getting older, and getting leaner and meaner. If he was going to do a man's work every day, perhaps he ought to have the freedom to express himself like a man, she reasoned.

Joe worked hard for the next few years, and the farm began to prosper. He became a father figure to his sisters, and Polly Ann made it a point to praise him often. She desperately hoped that his good efforts would continue.

Polly Ann's brothers heaped praise upon Joe and told him they appreciated his efforts to take care of his mother and sisters. Shortly after Joe turned sixteen, Polly Ann began hearing rumors about her son that disturbed her. She wondered if he was beginning to walk on the wild side, following in the footsteps of his father.

The first indicator came when a gossipy old woman whispered to Polly Ann while she was in Jacksonville one Saturday that Joe had "stayed over" at an older woman's house down by the Ocmulgee River ferry crossing when he was supposed to have slept at a cousin's house in town.

Polly Ann never asked Joe about that rumor. If she were to ask, Joe probably would tell her the truth, and she wasn't sure she was prepared to hear the truth. While she regarded her son as a grown man in some ways, she still wanted him to be her little boy in other ways. She was torn between asking and remaining silent, but she chose to put it out of her mind.

Another gossip told her Joe joined some older men at a flophouse down near the river and drank moonshine with them. Again, Polly Ann didn't bother to ask about the truth.

Instead, Polly Ann would tell anyone who would listen that her Joey was one of the hardest working young men in all of Telfair County. He certainly had kept that promise made on bended knee, and a mother in distress could hardly ask for more than that.

Even though there were other meetings between Carter and Joe, none of them turned violent. Joe never mentioned them to his mother, and Polly Ann, knowing that Carter had a reputation for being tough, hoped that they would not tangle again.

James Rawlins never returned to the cabin he'd built as a wedding gift for Polly Ann. Only once, about four years after he last visited the farm, did the family ever have any word about him. One of Polly Ann's brothers was traveling to Laurens County and, as he passed through the northern part of Telfair County, a merchant said James had visited his store a few weeks before.

Other than that, James Rawlins was nothing more than a distant memory in the lives of his wife and children. She dealt silently with her own misery. Joe worked hard and tried never to think about him. The older girls never mentioned him, and Mary was so young when he left that she would not have recognized her father if she had met him face to face.

2

JOE'S EDUCATION HAD MOVED FROM CLASSROOM TO FARM, and it turned out he was a better student on the farm than he ever had been in a classroom. He also proved that, despite his young age, he was a very smart trader when it came to farm animals. He always seemed to get top dollar when the family sold livestock, and Joe soon learned which animals were the best buys at the sales in Jacksonville.

Because of that, Polly Ann harbored no reservations about Joe's ability when it came time to buy a bull for breeding. She sent him to Coffee County to pick out a bull and pay for it, even though Joe was just seventeen. His mother's faith boosted his confidence, and he was an elated young man the morning he threw a raggedy old saddle on a horse and set out for Coffee County.

He rode Swains Ferry to the south bank of the Ocmulgee River that cold morning in January and went south on a twenty-six-mile trek along Old Blackshear Road. After spending the night in Broxton, Joe rode west the next morning to look for the farm of J. J. "Squire" Jowers. People in both Telfair and Coffee counties held Jowers in high esteem because he sold excellent livestock at reasonable prices. Folks in Broxton told him that the Jowers farm would not be difficult to find. Just take the road toward Ambrose, they said, and look for the biggest house in that part of the county.

Five miles into the countryside, Joe rode up a lane to the Jowers home and paused for a moment to admire the rambling Southern mansion. Joe soon learned that the man who lived there was just as Southern as the architecture of his house.

"Hello, young man, what brings you to my doorstep?" a voice boomed from inside the house.

"Came lookin' for breedin' stock," Joe called back.

A smiling man—indeed, a very big man physically—came out the front door and said, "You came lookin' at the right place, son."

A wide smile greeted Joe, and he smiled back. The man offered to shake hands—with his left hand. That's when Joe noticed that he had no right arm. His shirt was folded neatly around a nub and pinned back.

Joe reached out with his left hand and shook hands. They took an instant liking to one another.

"It's cold out here," Squire Jowers said. "Come in and sit for a spell. How about a cup of coffee?"

In the dining room, Jowers settled his large frame in a chair, smiled again and motioned Joe to a chair on the other side of the dining table. Then he asked, "Who's your pa, son?"

"That don't matter, sir," Joe said as respectfully as possible, considering the question. The smile disappeared from Joe's face as he said, "My Pa left...a long time ago. I do the farmin' and I do the buyin'."

Jowers sensed that he'd struck a raw nerve and he turned the conversation back to livestock. As they talked, the older man's admiration grew. Joe was indeed a knowledgeable young man, he soon learned.

After a few minutes, Jowers rose to his feet and said, "Let's go look at the bulls." But first, he said, he wanted Joe to meet his family. Rachel Jowers and several children filed into the dining room for a round of formal introductions. After Joe had acknowledged each of them, Jowers asked, "Where's Angeline?"

A voice from the kitchen said, "Comin', Pa." And then a girl of about seventeen appeared and Joe froze. He could only stare at the young woman in the doorway. Angeline Jowers, Joe quickly decided, was undoubtedly the most beautiful girl he'd ever seen.

Angeline stared back for a moment, then dropped her gaze and said softly, "Pleased to meet you," when her father introduced her as "my first born."

Both of Angeline's parents noted the exchange of glances by the two teen-agers. Rachel Jowers smiled. She knew romantic attraction when she saw it. Those two are star struck at first sight, she thought.

Immediately, Joe's mind went racing from one excuse to another for him to stay a while. He couldn't just take a bull and ride away without at least talking to Angeline for a few minutes.

He'd planned to start for home that afternoon, but he was having second thoughts. The farm back home would be all right without him for an extra day. Plowing wouldn't start for another three or four weeks. His only chores besides feeding the livestock were mending fences, sharpening plows, and such. Yes, another day here would be . . .

Squire Jowers broke into his thoughts.

"Cold ride coming this way, I'll bet."

"Yes, sir, real cold," Joe answered, his eyes still on Angeline. "I made it to Broxton yesterday afternoon, and I stayed overnight because I didn't know if I could find your place before dark."

"Well, you found it, and we're going to have something to eat shortly. Sure would be obliged if you would stay."

Joe's heart started thumping so loud he was sure the others could hear it. A team of horses couldn't have dragged him away. "Yes, sir, that'd be great! I'll stay. Yes, sir, I'll stay!"

Jowers pointed toward the back door of the house. "Livestock is out this way. Why don't we see if you can find a bull you'd be proud to own while Mrs. Jowers and Angeline put some food on the table?"

Joe followed the older man toward the back door, his gaze never leaving Angeline — until he ran into the doorjamb at the kitchen. Then, red-faced, he turned his head away from Angeline and followed the older man. He could hear laughter behind him.

Joe needed only a few minutes to pick out the bull he wanted. Jowers assured him that he'd made a good choice, and they went back into the house to escape the biting winter cold.

Several times during the noontime meal, the elder Jowers had to call Joe's name more than once to draw the young man's attention away from Angeline to answer a question. When they'd finished eating, Jowers said, "I think these two want to talk." And he shooed the other children away from the table, including Angeline's oldest brother, Gene, who was smirking and laughing at Angeline's obvious discomfort at being singled out in such a manner.

But she didn't object to her father's suggestion and in a few moments, Angeline and Joe were alone. Joe started to make small talk, but his first words came out as a squeak. Angeline laughed and carried some dishes to the kitchen while he tried to gain control of his voice. When she returned, he told Angeline all about his mother and three sisters, the family farm and the livestock. Finally, he ran out of words.

Before the silence became too uncomfortable, Angeline asked, "How come your Pa didn't come with you?"

Joe caught himself before making a sharp retort. He was the man of the house, he told her in a tone of finality.

Then he thought about what he'd just said, and he hastily added, "But I'm gonna get married some day and go out on my own. We've got the farm in good shape and the money situation is pretty good, too. Ma will be able to hire some help pretty soon, and then I can...."

He knew his face was reddening as he talked, but it seemed very important to him that Angeline should understand the situation fully—that he indeed would be free to get married in the near future.

They talked for half an hour before Rachel Jowers came into the dining room and told Angeline to help with the kitchen chores.

"And tell your brother not to tease you," she added. "If he does, tell him he'll be washing dishes for a week." An attractive woman at middle age, Mrs. Jowers sat down and regarded Joe for a moment. "Threatening Gene with having to wash dishes is the only way I can keep that boy in line sometimes. He's sixteen, and he'd rather plow all day than have to wash dishes."

Then she asked Joe about his mother and how she was doing. "I may have met your mother at the all-day Baptist gatherings. You say she goes to Blockhouse Church?"

Joe nodded.

"I think we've probably met," she said. "Would you take a message to her. Tell her I would like for the whole family to come down for a visit sometime."

Joe nodded vigorously that time. A visit by the family meant he would see Angeline again. Certainly, he would try to arrange that.

Finally, Joe excused himself and headed outside to look for Squire Jowers. He really ought to be leaving soon. He'd decided to spend another night in Broxton and then ride north the next day.

The older man hailed Joe from down near the barn. Jowers took him by the arm and said, "I want you to see my favorite horse." In the back stall of the barn, Joe saw a palomino, and it was surely the most beautiful horse he'd ever seen. Mr. Jowers seemed to be surrounded by beauty, Joe thought. Beautiful farm, beautiful wife, beautiful horse, and a beautiful daughter, too.

They stood on the leeward side of the smokehouse and talked about farming and horses and the best flavor of preserves to put on a cathead biscuit. In a very short time, the two had become friends.

Finally, Joe told the older man that he had enjoyed the visit, but that he ought to get started on the return trip. Then Jowers said something that made Joe's heart stop beating for a moment.

"Why don't you just stay here tonight," he said as more of a statement than a question. "You can get an early start tomorrow morning. There's a road going north from here that'll cut off a few miles and you won't have to go back through Broxton. You can make it home in a day, even leading a bull."

"Good idea," was all Joe's voice would let him say. How lucky could he be?

Joe rambled around the farm buildings, talked to a couple of Angeline's brothers and then sauntered back toward the house. Angeline was just coming out the back door as he approached.

He told her he was spending the night, and she said, "I know. I heard Pa tell Mama to fix you a bed."

Then she motioned him to follow her. "I know a nice place where we can talk," she said, "and it won't be too cold, either." And she led him to a sunny spot on the south side of the house. It was out of sight of the barn and blacksmith shop, and the young couple felt like they had a little privacy.

Joe just couldn't believe his good fortune. He'd found the most beautiful girl he'd ever seen and she *liked* him.

"I wish it was nicer weather," she said. "We could go for a horseback ride. There's a pond about a mile away, and I love to ride down to that place."

Joe made a promise to himself that he would go there one day with her.

Then he made the same promise to Angeline.

She smiled and said, "You gotta keep that promise, mister."

On the road to Jacksonville the next day, Joe's mind was filled with thoughts about what he would tell his mother. And when he wasn't arranging his speech to Polly Ann, he was enjoying the vision of Angeline smiling and waving good-bye as he rode away. The picture of her was engraved on his mind's eye, and nothing would ever erase it.

Joe arrived at the farm just before dark. He put the bull in a pen and filled a feed trough with grain. He was unsaddling his horse when it neighed and brought his mother out of the house.

"Why didn't you tell us you were home?" she asked.

"I wanted to get this done so we could talk."

As they walked toward the house, Polly Ann could sense an unusual excitement in her son, but he waited until they were inside the house and the girls were gathered around before he starting telling about his trip.

"I bought us a bull, and I'll show it to you in the morning," he said. "It was a long ride and it was cold...." His voice trailed off and everyone waited to hear what else he had to say.

"And I met the prettiest girl in the world," he went on, the words tumbling out like water from a broken dam. "Her name is Angeline Jowers. She's the daughter of the man who sold me the bull. She lives over by Broxton. On a big farm. With her parents, Squire and Rachel Jowers. I really like this girl. And she likes me, too!"

Polly Ann smiled. She was happy for her son, but Martha, oldest of his three sisters and Joe's best buddy, didn't seem thrilled in the least.

"What does this mean?" she asked. "Are you going to get married and move away?"

Joe stopped talking and was silent for a moment. "Well, Martha, you know I'm gonna do that some day...but I don't think it's gonna happen right away. I ain't but seventeen, and there's still a lot of work to be done here."

His voice trailed off again. He wasn't really sure what the future held. But he felt like it was brighter than it had been when he left three days before.

The next few weeks were a busy time as Joe worked to get everything ready for planting. Joe knew he had to do a good job. After the Civil War had ended and slaves were freed, not many farmers tried to grow cotton since a large labor force to harvest it was no longer available. Farmers in South Georgia were adjusting to the change, and most of them grew vegetables to sell or can and grain to feed the livestock.

The vegetable market had become very competitive, but Joe, born at the end of the Civil War, could not remember when it hadn't been that way. So he worked hard and produced the best crop he could, and he figured everything would take care of itself.

As the weeks dragged by, Joe longed to see Angeline, and Polly Ann knew it. She didn't want her son to rush into anything so serious as marriage, but she knew his feelings were strong. Joe and Angeline exchanged letters often, and she saw a relationship developing that took her back twenty years.

As soon as the planting was nearly complete, Polly Ann suggested that perhaps Joe should take a trip to Coffee County. Her son's face lit up at the suggestion, and even Martha seemed happy. She'd had some time to get used to the idea that her brother was going to marry and move away from the farm some day, and her desire to see him happy was more important to her than any loneliness she might feel when he was gone.

Joe worked right up until complete darkness each day, until every seed was in the ground. One morning in March, he saddled his horse well before daybreak and said good-bye at first light.

Once across the Ocmulgee River, Joe ran his horse as hard as he dared. He wanted to get to the Jowers farm at the earliest moment and have as much time as possible with Angeline.

The entire Jowers family welcomed Joe like a son who had been away for a while, and Angeline's brother, Gene, had some news for him. "All that sister of mine has done since you left is sit around and swoon," he said. "Ma gets after her all the time. She was sitting around last week, staring off into space, and she burned up a couple of pies. Pa threatened to send her off to Jacksonville just to see you so she could maybe straighten out her head!"

Joe managed to keep a check on his emotions that first night, but by the following morning, he was desperate for some time alone with Angeline. He had to know how she felt about him. So far, he had not mentioned marriage, but he was ready to talk about it and could hardly wait to see her reaction.

Joe was helping Mr. Jowers build a feed trough when Angeline came outside with a picnic basket and said, "If you'll hitch up the buggy, I'll show you that pond I told you about."

Mr. Jowers nodded his head toward the barn and said, "Go on." Less than fifteen minutes later, Joe and Angeline were riding down the road toward a creek that snaked across the Jowers holdings.

Their destination, the place Angeline had told him about, was indeed paradise. The weather had warmed considerably since his last visit, and they enjoyed a meal under a huge oak shade tree with Spanish moss hanging from every limb. Water gurgling over rocks in the stream played a melody for the young couple.

Eventually, Angeline packed everything back into the picnic basket and placed it in the buggy. But Joe wasn't ready to leave, and he indicated that by sprawling across the blanket that was still spread out on the ground. Angeline sat down beside him.

Joe looked into her big brown eyes and said, "I wanna tell you something, Angeline. Not one minute has passed since I first saw you that I haven't thought about you. A picture of you is right there before me all the time. If I couldn't think about you and plow a field, we wouldn't have a seed in the ground."

It was the longest speech, and surely the most earnest, he'd ever made to a girl. Angeline was flattered by what he'd said, and she told him so.

"I'll be eighteen in June, Angeline, and...." His voice failed once again and he paused. Then he blurted out, "And I want to marry you."

Angeline's gaze shifted from Joe's face to her hands. After a moment, she said, "Joe, I think you're great and I think I love you. But I need a little more time, and I need to talk to Mama. I told her that I thought this might get serious, but we didn't talk about a wedding and all. Let me talk to her."

Joe sighed in relief. She hadn't said no, and he felt good about that. So he could give her some time to think. That was no problem. But he was going to win her hand. He felt sure of that, even though his experience with girls was very limited.

Joe said his good-byes the next morning, saddled his horse at the stable and was riding around the house when Angeline suddenly burst through the front door and grabbed the bridle of his horse to stop him. She was breathless.

"I talked to Mama," she said, "She wants you to come back in the house and talk to Pa. If he says it's okay, we can get married!"

Joe dropped from the saddle and followed her into the house. Mr. Jowers came in the back door about that time, and the two men simply looked at one another for a few moments. Then Mr. Jowers said, "You want to talk to me, Joe?"

Joe could only nod. The time had come for him to be a man and ask for his true love's hand in marriage. He swallowed hard and began to speak. The older man sat across the dining table from him, and Joe talked earnestly about his feelings for Angeline. He talked until no more words would come. He stopped and waited, his heart pounding like a huge drum.

Mr. Jowers finally spoke. He said he thought a lot of Joe, admired his efforts to be a man and run his mother's farm. But was he ready for marriage? When he asked that question, Joe's heart dropped. Then Mr. Jowers said, "I think the two of you will be very happy. I'll set aside seventy-five acres for your own farm."

"Oh, no, Mr. Jowers," Joe said. "I'll work and pay for the land that Angeline and I farm." He paused a moment. "But I can't farm here in Coffee County right away. I'll have to give my Ma time to make arrangements for our farm. I'll have to talk to her."

Suddenly, the impact of Mr. Jowers' decision about his proposal for marriage hit him and he jumped up and said, "You said OK! You said OK!" And he let out a war whoop that could be heard a mile away.

"I gotta talk to Ma. I gotta go. Angeline, I love you."

He kissed her right there in front of everybody. Then he dashed outside and mounted his horse in a single bound. Angeline was running close behind him. She grabbed the reins of the bridle once more and said, "Mama wants you and your family to come and visit next week—to make plans for the wedding."

"We'll be here!" Joe shouted happily and, with a final wave of his hat at the Jowers family gathered on the porch, he sent his horse at a full gallop down the lane toward home. Another happy whoop echoed across the fields.

3

April 1883

EVERYTHING WAS READY FOR THE WEDDING. ANGELINE'S mother hand stitched every seam of a white wedding gown in just two weeks and trimmed it in lace. The big day — April 6, 1883 — arrived at last for the fidgety young couple. Families of both the bride and the groom gathered in the parlor of the Jowers home for a simple wedding ceremony. The bride was barely eighteen years old, and the groom was two months shy of that age. But both families joyously predicted a long and happy marriage for the handsome couple.

Joe and Angeline said their vows a little after one o'clock that warm spring afternoon, then celebrated with a huge wedding cake. Late in the afternoon, Joe drove his father-in-law's comfortable buggy into Broxton so he and Angeline could spend their wedding night at an inn. Mr. Jowers, who had treated Joe like a son from the beginning, already had taken care of arrangements for the honeymooners. They were lodged in the most elegant room at the inn and dinner was served in their room on a rolling cart that also carried a bottle of fine wine.

Neither Joe nor Angeline ever had drunk wine before, and it took only a few sips for each of them to become lightheaded. For a while, they talked hopefully about the future, about how many children they would have, about the kind of house they would build one day soon. They laughed as they recalled their first meeting, and Joe reminded

Angeline about how nervous he had been when it came time to talk to her father about marriage. Finally, the laughter subsided. They looked longingly at one another. Then they kissed passionately, shed all clothing and slipped into bed. The night was theirs.

The following morning, Squire Jowers drove the rest of the Rawlins family to Broxton, along with trunks packed with Angeline's clothes. Joe took the reins of the wagon team and bade farewell to his smiling father-in-law. As Jowers headed his buggy back toward his farm, Joe guided the Rawlins wagon out of Broxton on the road to Jacksonville.

Angeline knew that she and Joe were going to live with his family until Polly Ann could find someone to work her land on the halves. Polly Ann figured she could survive financially on half of what the crops from her land would bring, but she absolutely had to have Joe's help through that harvest season. Angeline wasn't thrilled at the idea of her and Joe living in the small cabin with four other people. It was sure to be crowded, and there would be very little privacy. Angeline longed for a home of her own. However, she understood Joe's commitment to his family and she admired him for it.

It wouldn't be long, she believed, until they would be back in Coffee County, living close to her parents and farming their own land. She was young and she was resilient. She knew she could survive the inconvenience of close quarters. The fact that she truly liked Polly Ann and the girls would make it easier for her.

But Angeline was not used to laboring in the fields. Back home, she had helped her mother with the cooking, cleaning and other household chores, and the outside work was left to her father, her brothers and the hired hands. But things were different on the Rawlins farm. Everyone had to pitch in. The work ethic—a do-any-job attitude—in the Rawlins family ran strong and, in time, Angeline could no longer ignore the need for her presence in the fields. So she went. Although her hands were soon covered with calluses from long hours of working with a hoe, she felt closer to Joe when they were working side by side.

Angeline wrote at least once every week to her mother and father, and she received a letter just about every week from them. But she did not have a chance to visit during the summer. To keep up such a farm without outside help, everyone worked six days a week unless rain stopped work in the fields. And, even if she were given the time to make a visit, Angeline would not have attempted the 25-mile trip without Joe at her side. Robbers and thugs waited along the rural roads in those days and presented a real danger to a woman traveling alone.

By mid-November, most of the crops were harvested and Joe sent Angeline's spirits soaring when he asked if she would like to visit her parents for Thanksgiving. She could hardly contain her happiness as Joe drove the wagon to Coffee County on Thanksgiving eve.

Joe and Angeline spent three days at the Jowers home, and it was one of the happiest times of their lives. The elder Jowers took the young couple to a section of land about a mile down the road and told them to pick out a site on which they would build their first home.

They chose a breezy rise in the rolling farmland, and that night, Joe, Angeline, and Angeline's parents sat at the dining table and worked on a floor plan for a two-bedroom house. When the pencil-drawn sketch was completed, Joe handed it to his father-in-law and said, "Why don't you smooth it out by the time we get back?"

Squire Jowers felt honored that Joe would trust the final draft of such an important document to him. And he said so.

Joe and Angeline returned to Jacksonville to hear some news that brought both joy and sadness to Joe. Polly Ann had worked out a deal with Abe Jones to work her farm on the halves in the coming year, and she would move into town so the Jones family could occupy the Rawlins cabin.

While it was good news for his marriage, it meant Joe soon would be leaving the only home he'd ever known. His childhood was forever rooted in that house and land. An empty feeling clutched his innards when he dwelled on the thought, so he tried to put it aside and enjoy his last month at home.

As Christmas neared, Angeline longed to be in Coffee County with her family, but Joe told her he wanted to spend this one last holiday season with his family. It probably would be their last together, he said. Angeline understood and wrote to her parents to say they would not arrive in Coffee County until after Christmas. However, the wait seemed worth it when she and Joe loaded the wagon the day after Christmas and headed for the Jowers home place.

As they rode along Old Blackshear Road, she talked happily about the house they planned to build – and about expanding it as children were born. Joe promised they would be living in it by the time spring planting started if he could get some help. Angeline looped her arm through his, and Joe whistled a tune as the wagon bumped along the road. She realized she'd never heard Joe whistle before. She knew that he, too, was very happy.

When they arrived at the Jowers place, Joe asked if he and Angeline could stay a few days until he found a temporary home while their house was being built. Mr. Jowers slapped his hands together and said, "No, I've got a better idea. I've already found a place where the two of you can stay."

He loaded them into the big buggy and drove them down the road that bordered the Jowers farm. As they approached the spot Joe and Angeline had picked for their first home, Angeline suddenly let out a squeal and said, "Papa, what have you done?"

There on the rise stood their dream house already completed. Tears of happiness rolled down Angeline's face as she jumped from the buggy and ran the last hundred yards to the house. As she dashed up the front steps and across the porch, Joe caught up with her. Before she could open the door, Joe scooped her up in his arms.

"Not so fast," he said. "This is a special day."

Then he carried her across the threshold.

Her parents followed them inside and Joe soon had a crackling fire going in the fireplace. They sat on brand-new furniture – some of it store-bought, some of it homemade and a few pieces of hand-me-downs – and they talked. Joe spoke admiringly of the handiwork that went into building the house and furniture, and Mr. Jowers's chest swelled with pride.

"Well, we're going to start on a barn next week," Mr. Jowers said. "And this time it won't be just me and the boys and the hired hands. This time, it will be *you* and me and the boys and the hired hands."

Joe wondered again how he had been so lucky as to wind up with a father-in-law like Squire Jowers.

When spring arrived, Joe Rawlins was elated to be finally planting his own crop. He labored with a zest he'd never felt before. The weather cooperated, and the planting was finished at an early date. Joe was indeed happy with his life.

Angeline also saw a softening in her husband's tough demeanor, and she liked that. The hard times of her husband's early life had instilled a toughness in him that made him reluctant to share some of his deepest thoughts with her. She was happy to see that invisible coat of armor around his feelings start to melt away as they sat on the porch and talked far into the night.

He seemed to hold her more tenderly each day, and she looked forward to his return from the fields each evening. She was an able cook and Joe put some pounds on his slender frame. He was growing into a very handsome young man, his face tanned and healthy, his body strong and capable for whatever task arose.

Joe's first efforts produced a bumper crop. Rain came when it was needed and stayed away when it was time to harvest. His hard work and good farming habits drew praise from friend and stranger alike.

Then another change came into Joe's life. He got religion. Joe never had attended church regularly in Telfair County. Angeline felt frustrated while they were living there because Joe always seemed to have an excuse for not going to church. While she and Polly Ann and the girls climbed into the wagon to make the trip to Blockhouse Church each Sunday, Joe would use any kind of excuse to stay behind. Sometimes, he'd work on Sunday, and that displeased both Angeline and Polly Ann. At other times, he simply said he was "too tired to go all the way to Blockhouse Church and listen to that preacher ramble for an hour and a half."

However, once they'd moved into their own home, Angeline became more insistent that he attend the twice-a-month services with her. She told Joe she did not like to travel alone, even on Sunday, and, if he didn't go, her parents would have to drive out of their way to pick her up and then take her back home. And she chided him that all of the other young wives had their husbands at their sides.

The congregation at New Hope Baptist Church just outside Ambrose gave Joe a warm welcome the first time he went there, and Joe quickly made friends with several young men his age. After a few Sundays, he stopped offering excuses for not going to church. He bought a Bible one Saturday in Broxton and started carrying it to church with him. He'd even quote a scripture now and then in his conversations with his in-laws. Squire Jowers, a deacon and charter member of the church, admired this change in his son-in-law, and he told other young men—and his sons, as well—that Joe Rawlins was just the sort of person they should admire and emulate.

And the more Joe was around Squire Jowers, the more he admired his father-in-law. In time, he heard the full story of how Mr. Jowers lost his arm.

He'd gone to war with Company A, 31st Georgia Regiment when he was just sixteen. His fifteen-year-old brother, John

Darling Jowers, had gone with him. Squire was wounded in the right arm at the second battle at Manassas on August 24, 1862, and he returned home to recover from his wounds.

A few months later, word reached Coffee County that his brother had been killed in combat. Squire, unable to cope at home with the loss of his favorite brother, voluntarily returned to the battlefront. He again was wounded in the right arm, this time at the battle of Gettysburg, and his right arm was amputated soon afterward. He was repatriated in a prisoner exchange the following month and returned to Georgia.

By the time he reached Coffee County that time, he was a battle-seasoned soldier at age twenty. A few months later, he married Rachel Cauley and built a log cabin for their first home. Despite the loss of his arm, Squire Jowers became a successful and respected farmer and rancher. He served a term as sheriff of Coffee County from 1877 to 1879. His influence on young men of the county was legend.

So it surprised no one when Squire Jowers led Joe to the ministry. On a crisp fall Sunday in 1884, Joe knelt with the preacher and his father-in-law and said he would dedicate his life to serving God. But the conversion was just the beginning of his religious odyssey.

Joe wanted more, and Mr. Jowers understood. He'd often described Joe as being "whole hog or none" in everything he did. So it didn't surprised him when Joe said he wanted to preach the gospel. Joe studied his Bible faithfully and he soon began filling in when the regular preacher was not available for the twice-a-month services at New Hope. He also helped conduct revivals at other churches, sometimes delivering moving sermons that drew praise from many quarters.

In May 1885, Joe was ordained by the South Georgia Conference. A couple of weeks later, Angeline told him he was going to be a father.

On December 30, 1885, Milton Newton Rawlins was born. Joe proudly held the dark-haired baby and made his wife and baby the same promise he'd made to his mother half a dozen years before—that he would take care of them and never forsake them like so many men, including his own father, had done to their families.

Joe became a dedicated father, and it seemed he could not spend enough time with Milton. From the time the boy could walk, Angeline would say, "He not only looks like you, Joe, but he walks like you. Look at him!"

That made Joe very proud.

In ensuing years, Joe's farm prospered. His acreage grew from seventy-five to a hundred and fifty and then to more than two hundred. He hired a couple of field hands and built modest houses for them on his land.

Several years passed before Joe returned to Jacksonville to see his mother and sisters. They had exchanged letters every few weeks, but this was the first time in years he'd had a chance to sit down and talk face to face with Polly Ann and the girls.

All three of his sisters were married and Martha had a child of her own. The impromptu reunion with all of her children made Polly Ann Rawlins very happy. As it turned out, that would be the last gathering of all of them. Martha died a couple of years later while she was helping her husband burn stumps. Her dress caught afire and she panicked. By the time her husband caught up with her and put out the fire, the burns were so severe that she never recovered.

While visiting friends in Jacksonville on that first trip back, Joe learned something that did not put a smile on his face. His old enemy, William L. Carter, had bought land in Coffee County and was moving there with his wife and baby, Joe was told. Joe didn't know that Carter was, at that moment, breaking ground for a new house less than a mile from his own home. But he found out soon after he returned home.

The morning after his return, Joe saw a wagonload of lumber passing along the road and he could see that it turned onto the land bordering his place. He wondered who was building there, and he decided to ride that way and welcome his new neighbors. But, as Joe approached, he recognized W.L. Carter. He never uttered a word. He simply turned his horse and rode away.

Joe did not mention Carter—or the previous trouble he'd had with him—to Angeline that night, but as they ate their evening meal, Angeline sensed something was wrong. But she couldn't get Joe to open up and talk about it.

Joe did not want to trouble his wife. She was close to delivering their second child, and he didn't want to upset her. He told her it was nothing important, and he sat there afterward, holding his son close and trying to enjoy being back home. But thoughts of this new neighbor nagged at him. Joe decided he would not tell Angeline about feuding with Carter until after the baby came.

On April 19, 1888, and in the midst of the planting season, Leonard Rawlins was born. A second healthy son made Joe very happy, and he tried not to think about Carter living just down the road.

On a couple of occasions, Joe and W.L. were in Broxton at the same time, but they did not meet directly and Joe breathed a sigh of relief. His conversion to Christianity had changed his life, and he dreaded the thought of any confrontation with his old enemy. He was content to just let it rest.

But the old animosity came flooding back soon after Joe heard an announcement in church that both W.L. Carter and his wife, Ella, were sick and spring planting at his farm was far from completed. Even though the Carters attended a different church, the Jowers family always tried to help neighbors when they needed help regardless of their religious affiliation.

Joe voiced reluctance to go to Carter's place. "I had trouble with Carter back in Jacksonville," he said. "And there could be real trouble if I show up over there."

Jowers assured him everything would be all right, that he would handle any problems that arose. Besides, Jowers said, "This might be the chance for the two of you to bury the hatchet."

Joe didn't think so, but he gave in to his father-in-law's wishes and the next day, he joined a dozen men driving wagons loaded with farm implements to the Carter place. But Carter gave them a cold reception. "I didn't ask for this help," he said from his porch. "Y'all can do it if you want, but I don't want any help from that damned Rawlins trash."

Joe started to climb down from the wagon seat and find out just how sick Carter really was, but his father-in-law, who was already on the ground, pushed Joe back inside the wagon.

"You take a couple of hands and go down to that back field and plant the cotton," Jowers said to Joe. "I'll take care of matters here."

Joe stifled the urge to just drive away and let Carter fend for himself. His relationship with his father-in-law was more important than anything Carter might say about him.

The volunteers worked hard for two days to catch up on Carter's planting, and not once did Carter appear to encourage them or express any measure of gratitude. After they returned to their own farms, the volunteers expected Carter would come by one day and thank them for their help. But he never did, and Carter became a sullen outcast in that part of Coffee County.

Carter was a mystery man in the county. Few people got to know him, and only sketchy details about his past ever came to light. He bought and sold land, and once told one of the merchants that he owned land in half a dozen places. Carter was known to be a Methodist preacher, and he had a similar background to another preacher, namely Joe Rawlins.

His father returned from the Civil War a very sick man. He died just a few months after arriving back at the family farm near Oglethorpe in Macon County. Young Willie Carter, like

Joe Rawlins, went through a tough growing-up period without a father to influence and guide him. He did not marry and father children until he was nearly thirty years old.

Carter also told the preacher at his church that it was "a weird twist of fate" that he happened to buy land bordering on Rawlins' place. Of course, Rawlins did not see it that way. He believed that Carter was following him around and trying to make life difficult for him.

Carter's lack of gratitude for the help planting his crops was not the end of that matter. Several weeks later, Carter and the elder Jowers met at the general store in Broxton. Carter's first words were, "That damned Rawlins boy planted my cotton in the wrong field."

Squire Jowers drew in a deep breath and said, "I told him where to plant it, Mr. Carter. So don't blame him. Besides, you weren't a whole lot of help while we were there. We tried to do the neighborly thing and you've never once uttered a word of thanks."

Carter opened his mouth as if to say something, but he felt that every eye in the store was fixed on him, and there wasn't a friendly expression in the place. He'd obviously picked the wrong man—indeed, a very popular man—to rail at. He suddenly said, "All of you can just go to hell. Stay off my land from now on."

"That," said Squire Jowers testily, "will not be a problem."

When Joe heard about the exchange, he was—for the first time in a long time—mad enough to go after Carter. Instead, he buried his anger deep inside and let it stay there. However, he knew he had not seen nor heard the last of W.L. Carter.

Several months later, a neighbor hailed Joe and stopped to talk on the road to Ambrose. The neighbor said Carter had made some pretty loose remarks about Angeline in Broxton a few days before. The neighbor said, "Carter even went so far as to say he'd bet she'd make a fine bed partner. He also said that anyone named Rawlins wouldn't know about making a woman happy."

Joe bit his lip and again tried to let it go. He decided not to go after Carter right away. He'd wait to see if that was a one-time incident or if Carter would continue with his poisonous words. Joe thought he'd made the right decision. Some of Joe's fellow church members said they heard what Carter had said and that they admired Joe for keeping his temper in check. Their praise sustained Joe a little longer.

4

W.L. Carter built a reputation in Coffee County for being a ladies' man, and Joe soon learned that Angeline was not the only target for his trashy talk. He dropped the names of other women, and his comments were often the basis for some pretty racy rumors.

Joe felt a little better, knowing that Angeline was not Carter's only target. Maybe someone else would settle with Carter first, maybe even run him out of the county. But before that could happen, Joe created a crisis of his own.

One warm June day, Joe was rounding up stray calves when he saw Angeline coming out of the woods that lined the creek near the property line between the Rawlins and Carter farms. He knew that one of Angeline's sisters had come over for the day to help look after the children, but he didn't understand why his wife was so far from the house. Just as he started to call her name, he noticed Carter leaving the same wooded area in another direction.

Joe's temper exploded for the first time in years. He spurred his horse into a gallop directly at Angeline and then reined it to a halt in front of his startled wife. He dropped quickly to the ground, and a smile that started on Angeline's face quickly vanished when she saw the stormy expression on her husband's face.

"What's wrong?" she asked.

"What the hell were you doin' in the woods . . ."

His voice stopped abruptly. Joe gestured to the skirt of her dress. "What the hell are pine needles doing all over your dress?"

"I decided to walk down here and rest while Sarah played with the children."

Joe grabbed her arm roughly and said, "And who were *you* playin' with?"

Angeline tried to pull her arm free of Joe's grasp. She'd never seen him like this. There was an insane expression in his eyes, unmasked anger on his face.

"I wasn't playing with anyone. What's the matter with you, Joe?"

Joe pointed to the distant figure. "What were you and Carter doin' down there in the woods *together*?"

"Joe, we were *not* together. I never saw him down there, never spoke to him. Now let go of me!"

For a moment, Joe loosened his grip on her arm. She pulled her arm free and started to turn away. Tears welled in her eyes.

Joe grabbed her arm and turned her to face him again. "Let me set your mind straight about somethin', Angeline," Joe said, his voice low and threatening. "If I ever find you beddin' down with another man, I'll fix you so no man will ever look at you again. And if I ever find out you've bedded down with that son-of-a-bitch W.L. Carter, I'll kill you and him!"

Joe's eyes still blazed with anger as he turned away, mounted his horse and rode away.

Angeline looked after her husband, tears flowing freely down her cheeks. She had never seen her husband fly into such a jealous rage. She did not understand what prompted the outburst, but as she dried her tears, she vowed to find out.

Joe did not mention the scene in the field to her that evening. He didn't mention Carter's name, either. But he turned a cold shoulder to her when they were in bed at night.

Angeline felt an aching hurt, a loneliness that she'd never known before, especially with Joe lying next to her.

After church the following Sunday, Joe, Angeline, and the boys ate the afternoon meal with her parents, and Angeline made it a point to get her father alone long enough to tell him what had happened and ask what he knew about W.L. Carter.

Squire Jowers told his daughter about the planting incident and said that Joe and Carter had "crossed swords" back in Telfair County. But even her father was at a loss to explain the unbridled anger and outright hatred Joe obviously felt for W.L. Carter.

After supper that evening, Joe seemed to be more like his old self, and Angeline decided to have a talk with him.

"Tell me what's going on, Joe, between you and Carter," she said.

Joe's temper didn't show this time, but his explanation was short. "He and my Pa had problems. Then me and him fought a couple of times."

Joe grew silent.

"But you can get over that, can't you?"

"One thing I won't ever get over is him lyin' about my family."

"What did he lie about?"

"Carter said my Pa stole some of their hogs, but the sheriff found out the hogs had been sold—by Carter himself—to a fella across the river. That made him out to be a liar in front of the whole population of Jacksonville—and Telfair County, too, I guess. Anyhow, I kept having trouble with him after Pa left. And it never stopped until I moved down here. I was hoping I'd seen the last of him. But now it's started all over again. I may have to kill him."

Cold chills ran up Angeline's spine at that pronouncement. She reminded Joe of his Christian beliefs.

Again Joe fell silent. He thought about telling her what Carter had said about her in Ambrose, but he suddenly rose to his feet and walked outside.

Angeline decided it might be best to just let it rest. If indeed it would.

She still didn't know how deeply the hatred ran between her husband and their neighbor. But she would soon find out.

Several weeks later, Joe and Angeline left the children at the Jowers place and rode to Broxton in a new buggy Joe had bought for Angeline. After tethering the team near the center of town, they had split up, Joe going to the hardware store and Angeline walking to a dress shop down the street. As Angeline came out of the dress shop, she ran almost head-on into W.L. Carter. The sudden face-to-face meeting obviously flustered Angeline, but Carter, a tall man with angular features, smiled like he'd just met an old friend.

"Howdy, Miz Rawlins," he said. She started to go around him, but he put his hand on her arm and said, "Hey, talk to me. We've never had a chance to say hello. Lived right down the road from one another for years and never had a chance to say a word. Say, you're plumb cute. If you ever get a chance –"

Angeline had not noticed her husband's hasty approach, and apparently, neither had Carter. Angeline suddenly heard a sickening thud as Joe's fist collided with the side of Carter's jaw. Carter spun backward and fell face down. Joe grabbed Angeline's arm in a viselike grip and yanked her down the boardwalk toward their buggy.

As people stared, Angeline tried to calm her husband. "Joe, what is the matter with you?" she asked in as much of a whisper as she could. "Let go of my arm!"

Joe suddenly slapped her hard across the left cheek. Angeline tried to pull loose from him, but he savagely struck her again. "You'd better quit fighting me, damn it, or I'm going to –"

That time, he didn't finish what he was saying. He heard his name called and he turned to see Carter with a double-barrel shotgun leveled at him. "Rawlins, I think it's time I killed you!"

Joe calmly held his hands away from his sides. "Gonna shoot an unarmed man, Carter? You'll wind up on the end of a rope for that."

Before he could say any more, several men intervened and took the gun from Carter. He was told to go home and cool off. Others surrounded Rawlins while Carter was driving his wagon out of town. Carter's previous remarks about Angeline were common knowledge among the town's citizens, and they didn't blame Joe for slugging Carter. But they didn't want to see anyone get killed.

Joe was still in a huff. He grabbed Angeline's arm again and half-walked, half-dragged her to the buggy some fifty feet away. Then he shoved her up against the side of the buggy and reached inside. Bringing out a rope used to lead horses behind the buggy, he looped it around Angeline's neck and said, "You're going to learn about me and Carter. You're going to learn if it kills you. Or me. Or both of us."

"What are you doing, Joe? Have you lost your mind?"

"Carter's got a reputation for being a ladies' man," Joe hissed, his voice filled with hate. "Well, if you're gonna graze with the bulls, I figure I might as well lead you home like a cow in heat."

Angeline reached to pull the rope from her neck. Joe slapped her again. "Don't even think about it," he said.

"Oh, my God, Joe, you've lost your mind!" Then she said it even louder, "You've lost your mind!" And tears began streaming down her cheeks.

A couple of men approached with the obvious intention of interceding, but Joe suddenly pulled a shotgun from beneath the seat of the buggy, cocked the hammer and said, "This ain't your affair. Keep out of it."

As they backed off, Joe held the gun trained in the direction of the onlookers as he stepped into the driver's seat and drove the buggy out of town at a walk with Angeline tied behind it. Angeline was forced to run a few steps now and then to keep up. After the buggy turned on the road toward home and they pulled out of sight of the businesses, Joe reined the horse to a halt and turned to Angeline. "Get on the back of the buggy," he said. "You can ride from here. I think you've learned your lesson."

Of course, word about that incident quickly reached Squire Jowers and he wasted no time in dispatching Gene to summon Joe and Angeline to the big house.

When they arrived, Jowers motioned them to seats in the dining room. They sat at the same table where they'd eaten their first meal together, where they'd planned their wedding, where they'd drawn up plans for their home.

"I want to hear what both of you have got to say. Ladies first, Angeline."

Angeline told about her sudden meeting with Carter and how Joe had reacted. She didn't mention being led out of town like a cow. She was sure her father already knew about that, and since it was the most demeaning experience of her life, she had no desire to rehash it.

Joe didn't want his father-in-law meddling in his affairs, but he was indebted to the old man and he respected the war hero. In his defense, he told how he'd "caught" Angeline coming out of the woods a few weeks before and that Carter was leaving the woods in another direction. He admitted he was insanely jealous of his wife and would summarily kill any man who tried to take her away from him.

Squire Jowers leaned back in his chair and said, "I know about your background, Joe, and I know it put a mean streak in you. But I've seen things in war that you'll never see, and I suppose that put a little meanness in me, too. Even so, I've never taken it out on womenfolk. I've never hit a woman in my life, never even felt the need or the urge."

He paused and let his words sink in. Then he went on, "I raised Angeline to be a lady, and I don't see where you have any real proof that she has been anything else. If she ever goes bad, I'll be just as quick to disown her as you would. I think you'd better cool off and think real hard about this."

He hesitated for a moment but neither of the young people moved. "I'm going to say one more thing. The Jowerses have a reputation in this area for being kind, gentle, reverent, hard-working people. Joe, you seemed to want to be one of us from the first time you came here, and I've treated you like my own son. Don't embarrass me with any more shenanigans. Understand?"

Joe nodded. He went home and sat in a chair far into the night. Two emotions coursed through him as he sat there. He wanted to make up with his wife...and he wanted to kill W.L. Carter.

Just a year after Leonard was born, Angeline brought Joe a third son. Jesse Rawlins made his earthly debut on May 6, 1889. As he held his newborn, Joe, who had long since mended fences with his wife, smiled at Angeline and said, "This is the third son. Don't you think it's about time you had a girl?"

Eventually, two daughters were born, Leila on Sept. 11, 1890, and Lola on March 24, 1892.

Joe loved those girls, but his sons were his heartbeat. They followed him everywhere, and, even though there were differences in their looks—Milton and Jesse were dark headed like Joe but Leonard had a shock of hair the color of corn tassels—they all walked and talked like their old man.

He taught all of them to hunt and fish, and they often accompanied their father to the woods and streams. Although he tried to treat them all the same, he was closest to Milton, his first born.

Milton was about eight years old when his father taught him to swim. "I want you to learn real good so you can look after your brothers," he said. The first time Milton tried to swim all the way across the pond, he sank. Joe pulled him from the water and held his trembling body close.

"I thought I was going to drown, Pa," Milton sputtered. "I thought I was gonna die for sure."

"I'm not gonna let anything happen to you," his father said. "My job is to take care of you and teach you, and I'll always do that. It's kind of the way life is, son. I take care of you when you're young and, when you grow up, you take care of me when I'm old."

Milton left the pond that day feeling closer to his father than ever. And he was sure his father had saved his life.

During one hunting trip, Milton asked Joe if his father had ever taken him hunting.

"Many times," said Joe, the memories rushing back. "We used to trap furs along the river and trade them for things we didn't grow on the farm."

Then Milton asked why he never saw his grandfather. Joe thought about telling him that the old man had died, but he decided to tell the truth. With his voice sometimes choked with emotion, Joe told Milton about how his father deserted the family when he was just twelve and how he started farming full time when he was thirteen.

After he finished telling the story, he added, "But I won't ever leave you or Mama or any of the children."

Every detail of what Joe said was etched forever in Milton's mind and, later, he would tell the story to his younger brothers so his father wouldn't have to answer those questions again.

By the summer of 1892, Joe was farming three hundred acres, and the crops were so good that he was ready to pay off the land at the end of the harvest. He'd put the feud with Carter out of his mind, and he began preaching revivals in other towns. But he didn't really believe the trouble with W.L. Carter was over. And it wasn't.

One afternoon, Joe arrived at the Jowers farm all covered with dust and told his father-in-law that Carter had tried to run his buggy off the road with a team of mules and a big wagon. "Scared the little filly half to death," he said and then paused. "If I stay around here and he does, too, I'm goin' to have to kill him. I try to live by the scripture, but I keep comin' back to the one that talks about an eye for an eye and a tooth for a tooth."

Squire Jowers urged Joe to live like a Christian and keep a cool head. Shortly after that, the feud heated up again. The two men went to court several times, one accusing the other of trespassing, stealing farm animals or some other transgression. Joe told his father-in-law that he was fed up with the whole situation.

"I'm thinkin' about lookin' somewhere else," he said. "Maybe if we move away from here, Angeline and I can find peace. The kids are gettin' older, and they don't need to be mixed up in this fightin' all the time."

The possibility that Joe might move away tugged at the old man's heartstrings. Angeline was his oldest child and her children were his first grandchildren. He adored those children—especially the three boys—and took great pride in influencing them as much as he could.

However, if Joe thought moving away might solve his problems with Carter—which was the only problem he had in Coffee County—then Jowers said he would buy Joe's land and help any way he could. Once again, Joe was humbled by his father-in-law's generosity and understanding.

A few days later, Joe rode westward. He was gone for five days, and when he came back, he said he'd found a paradise in northern Lowndes County near Hahira.

"It's eleven hundred acres of the prettiest land you'll ever see," he told a gathering at his father-in-law's house. "Only about three hundred are cleared for farmin'. But the woods and swamps are great for fishin' and huntin'. The boys will love this place."

Then he looked at his wife and said, "Angeline will like it, too."

He could afford the larger place, he said, because the house on the property was old and in disrepair. But he could remedy that with hard work, and then he would build a new house as soon as he could afford it.

Even though Angeline was not looking forward to living in a house that was little more than a barn, she was willing to try just about anything to put some serious miles between her husband and W.L. Carter.

5

JOE AND HIS HIRED HANDS WORKED HARD TO COMPLETE THE fall harvest, and then, one day in early November, Joe and his family loaded their possessions into four wagons. Joe took the reins of one with twelve-year-old Milton at his side. Squire Jowers, his boys and one of the hired hands drove the other wagons. Angeline drove the buggy with the other four children and her fragile items—dishes, lamps and such—loaded in back.

The fifty-five-mile trip took three very long days, but when the Rawlins family finally arrived at the farm just off Val Del Road about eleven miles north of Valdosta, they received the warmest welcome newcomers could expect anywhere. A small army of neighbors was on hand to greet the wagon train.

In fact, the neighbors already had cleaned out the house, washed the walls and made it as livable as possible. Someone had fashioned a spit and placed it over the blacksmith's forge. A hog was being barbecued, and early that evening, everyone sat down to eat fresh pork, vegetables and pie brought from the homes of others. Joe and Angeline felt certain they'd found the perfect place to settle.

Mr. Jowers and the boys stayed an extra day to look around, talk with the neighbors and build an outhouse with lumber donated by the neighbors. When Squire Jowers rode away the following morning, he felt good about where his grandchildren would live. Joe had made a good choice.

Before the cold January wind began to blow, the Rawlinses—with the help of neighbors—had completed repairs to the house, and it grew more comfortable almost daily. Two smaller rooms were added for the children's beds, and by spring planting time, the house was spacious enough and warm enough to keep Angeline happy.

Joe wanted for nothing that first spring in Lowndes County. If the right plow wasn't on hand at his place or if he needed seed or if he needed a hand, it seemed that someone was always close at hand. And Joe didn't forget their kindness. He told them to invite their friends to hunt and fish on his land.

And when the first cold came almost a year after the Rawlinses had moved to the area, Joe killed a hog, barbecued it, and invited everyone who'd helped him get settled and make that first crop of corn, cotton, peanuts and tobacco. In less than a year, he had become one of the most popular figures in the area.

In the next three years, Joe's reputation as a generous man grew, and so did his army of friends. When he saw children walking to school, he often picked them up in his wagon or buggy and delivered them right to the schoolhouse door. His boys were getting old enough to do a man's labor each day, and they often helped neighbors during time of sickness and death.

For Angeline, life was wonderful. The only thing that bothered her was her husband's lack of fervor for church life. She reasoned that perhaps he just missed his friends at New Hope. But he stopped preaching altogether, never offering to fill in for a sick preacher or help with revivals.

Angeline also saw occasional flashes of Joe's more temperamental ways. Sometimes he punished the children, especially the boys, much more harshly than she thought was necessary. She wondered if he would be so heavy-handed if her father was still close by. If she said something about the harshness of the punishment, Joe would fly off the handle and rail at her. After a while, she stopped questioning his methods.

But if his temperament had slipped a little, his farming skills certainly had not. He was a firm believer in the use of compost for fertilizer, and his crops thrived. His harvest always was among the best in the Hahira area.

The children attended a good school just over a mile away, and Angeline reached a comfort zone in Lowndes County that she had not known in years.

In 1902, Joe Rawlins' sons ran all the way home from school to tell their father that W.L. Carter, Joe's long-time antagonist, had bought the old Meadows place and was moving in. The Carter children had enrolled in school that morning, they said. Joe was flabbergasted. He looked at Angeline and said, "Why? Just tell my why?"

Angeline looked stunned. She slowly shook her head.

"Gene said last summer that Carter moved to Florida," Joe went on. "Why in the world would he move here?"

Angeline tried to smile at her husband as she said, "Maybe he'll just stay away." But in her heart, she didn't believe that. Neither did Joe.

"The Meadows place touches ours down there in the woods," he said. "I'll bet that son-of-a-bitch will trespass every day to hunt and fish on our land. But it ain't gonna happen. I'll settle this right now."

Angeline started to chide him about his language, but then she saw that Joe was reaching to the top of a kitchen cabinet and taking down an oak box. He opened it, removed a .32 caliber revolver and checked the load.

Angeline put her hand over the hand holding the pistol and said, "No, Joe, let's don't go looking for trouble. Please?"

"To hell with that. I'm goin' over there and let Carter know that if he starts one damn thing with me, then he's a dead man."

"Please, don't take that pistol."

Joe's mouth curled into a grin but his eyes were as cold as ice when he said, "If I don't need it, I won't use it. But if I need it, then Carter is on his way to hell. Today."

He strode out of the house, saddled his horse at the barn and rode down the lane toward the Meadows place.

Even as Joe was riding in his direction, W.L. Carter was talking to Tim McDonald, who owned a sliver of land between the Rawlins and Carter farms. McDonald asked Carter if he knew Joe Rawlins. Carter seemed surprised and said, "Sure hope it ain't the Joe Rawlins I know, the one from Coffee County."

They were still talking when Joe rode up to the Meadows place. Joe didn't waste any time in delivering his message. He hit the ground and confronted Carter with a murderous expression on his face and told him to leave. "Just pack up and go, you scoundrel. I've found peace in this place and, if you don't get out of your own accord, I'm going to run your sorry ass and all of your family out of Lowndes County."

McDonald was taken aback and Joe noticed it. "Me and this son-of-a-bitch have fought for years, Tim. He will lie with his every breath. He wouldn't know the truth if he heard it. Be careful with this rascal. He's a real snake."

Joe turned back to Carter and said, "Are you gonna go or do I have to run you out?"

Carter smirked and challenged him to carry out the threat.

The demeanor of the two men that day mirrored events that were to follow. Joe Rawlins was bossy, menacing and hateful toward Carter. On the other hand, Carter was stubborn, taunting and demeaning toward Rawlins. Later, he would brag that he alone had run Rawlins out of Coffee County.

After their confrontation, Joe arrived back at his house with a worry cloud over him that Angeline had not seen in years.

"Well, just ignore him, and maybe everything will work out," she said.

"That ain't gonna happen," Joe said. "This time, I will have to kill him. That's for damn sure."

For a while, it appeared that Joe Rawlins might keep the peace. In fact, Angeline even rejoiced when her husband harshly disciplined their sons over an incident at the swimming hole.

One hot spring day, Joe told his sons they could quit early and go swimming in the pond at the back of the property where it bordered the Carter farm. When the boys arrived at the pond, they found one of Carter's children, Willie, swimming there. While the Carter boy splashed about, the Rawlins boys quietly stole his clothes and hid them so he would have to go home naked.

With the boys' unexpected return to the home place, Joe asked his sons why they weren't still swimming. The boys bragged about what they had done. Joe gave each of them a whipping and sent them to get the clothes and take them to the Carter house.

But Joe's effort to try to do the right thing didn't cool hostilities between the men. Carter told neighbors that the Rawlins boys were bullies and that they had beaten his son with a stick at the swimming hole. Joe's boys denied any such attack on Willie Carter.

"Why does he always have to lie about us?" he asked Angeline. Then he walked over to Tim McDonald's house and asked his neighbor, who still had a talking relationship with Carter, to go to the Carter house and see if there were any marks on the Carter boy. McDonald rode up to the Rawlins house a couple of hours later and told Joe that Carter had ordered him off his property, that Carter believed he was there just to spy for the Rawlinses.

Joe openly cursed Carter, and his boys heard the whole thing. So they soon took up the feud, knowing that their father probably would approve anything they did.

At school one day, Milton taunted Willie, the oldest boy among Carter's children, and tried to draw him into a fight. The Carter youngster refused, saying that Milton was three years older and much bigger than he was. When Milton heard that, he turned to Jesse, his youngest brother who was the same age and about the same size as Willie, and said, "Kick his butt, Jesse." Jesse wasted no time in giving the Carter boy a sound thrashing.

Jesse was sent home for fighting, but he wore the suspension like a badge of honor. He proudly told his father why he was sent home. This time, the old man offered a different reaction than he had over the clothes-stealing incident. Looking at twelve-year-old Jesse with those piercing eyes, he only asked, "Did you whup him real good?"

"Yeah, Pa, he didn't put up much of a fight. He was bleedin' from the nose and mouth when it was over."

"Well," Joe said, his chest swelling with pride, "you ain't in no trouble with me, son. In fact, if you'll remind me the next time we go to town, I'll buy you one of those quarter bags of candy for doin' such a good job."

When Milton arrived at home later that day and heard about Jesse's reward, he said, "Hey, Pa, what about me? I put Jesse up to whuppin' that Carter kid."

"OK," his father answered, "you get a quarter bag of candy, too."

Two days later, a deputy sheriff arrived at the Rawlins farm with a court summons.

"I hate to do this, Joe," said the deputy, who had hunted birds and other game on the Rawlins farm, "but the magistrate wants you to bring Jesse in to the next term of court. I'm sure it won't be nothing but a warning. I'm just doing my duty, Joe. You understand that?"

"Sure," said Joe. "We'll be there. I want to see what old Carter has cooked up this time."

Just as the deputy had predicted, Jesse got nothing more than a stern warning for the fight. In fact, the magistrate, who came to hold court at the little courthouse on Val Del Road, criticized the schoolteacher for not "handling the matter at school instead of taking up valuable court time with such a trivial matter."

However, Carter did not take the court's decision quietly. He rose to his feet and railed against the Rawlinses, saying they were thieves and bullies. Before the magistrate could quiet his loud ranting, Carter stated that Jesse was "a hooligan just like his daddy and granddaddy," and he repeated his charge of long ago: that the boy's grandfather had stolen hogs from him twenty-five years before.

At that pronouncement, Joe Rawlins lunged at Carter, but deputies kept them apart. The magistrate threatened to fine both men if they did not settle down and keep their children under control, too.

Deputies made sure that the two families left by different routes that afternoon.

But the feud was raging.

Acrimony between the two families became as commonplace as the common cold. In early 1903, the Carters and the Rawlinses were in and out of court several times. In one case, the Rawlins boys chased a Carter cow that had strayed into their crops, tied shucks to its tail and set the shucks on fire. Carter hauled Joe Rawlins into court, saying that the Rawlins children had "ruined a good milk cow."

But Joe was popular with people throughout the county, including many court officials. The judge fined Joe Rawlins $10 for his sons' cruelty to animals and warned him once again to control his sons. But he declined to give Carter any monetary settlement.

In the summer of 1903, Carter brought criminal charges against the Rawlins boys, saying they had tried to drown his son, Willie, who was fourteen. Milton Rawlins, then seventeen and as big and tough as most men, told the magistrate at a hearing that the Carters constantly trespassed on Rawlins land and that Willie Carter had been told previously to stay out of the "swimming hole" at a creek that ran through Rawlins property.

"We ain't tried to drown that boy, sir," Milton said. "If we'd wanted to drown him, we coulda done that. There was three of us, and he couldn't have put up much of a fight. We just wanted to scare him away. Talkin' to him hadn't done no good at all."

The magistrate dismissed the charges and told Carter to keep his children off Rawlins land.

Later that year, the two men argued over a property line where their farms met at the south end of the Rawlins property. Again, Carter was a loser. The property line on the deed was quite clear, and the judge dismissed the case.

Outside the courtroom in rural Lowndes County that afternoon, Joe Rawlins, who had begun carrying a pistol regularly, drew the gun on W.L. Carter and threatened to kill him. Carter tried to have Rawlins arrested, but Sheriff J. F. Passmore had grown so tired of the constant bickering between the two men that he refused to seek a warrant or even send a deputy to dress down Rawlins for drawing the pistol.

He told Carter, "You've had Rawlins in court half a dozen times, and you've haven't won the first round. Leave the man alone, and maybe he'll leave you alone."

For a while in the fall of 1904, Joe Rawlins enjoyed a respite from trouble when W.L. Carter got into a row with another neighbor. Carter brought charges against two sons of

Tim McDonald, who owned ten acres of property sandwiched between the farms of Carter and Rawlins.

On September 10, 1904, McDonald's boys appeared in court for shooting Carter's guineas. Carter accused the McDonald boys of entering his yard and killing the guineas as his wife protested.

After Carter told his version of the conflict from the witness stand, McDonald testified that he'd had problems for months with Carter's guineas getting into his cornfield and digging up seed. He testified that he told Carter on two occasions to keep his guineas on his own property, and warned him on the second occasion that, if it happened again, the guineas would be shot. When it happened a third time, he said that he and his sons shot thirteen of the guineas, all of them in the McDonald corn patch.

When Magistrate J.B. Wilkinson called Carter back to the witness stand to explain why their versions differed on where the shooting took place, Carter said again that the boys had entered his yard and killed the guineas there. At that point, McDonald rose from his seat and said, "Don't swear to that statement, Mr. Carter, for you know it is not true."

Carter again repeated the statement and McDonald rushed toward him with a knife in hand. A large crowd had gathered at the rural courthouse to hear the case, and a collective gasp went up.

Carter ducked his head at the last moment, and the slash that was aimed at his throat only punctured the side of his neck below the ear. The stab wound grazed the jugular vein but did not cut it. If it had, little could have been done to keep Carter from bleeding to death.

Even so, the wound was serious enough that court was adjourned while Carter sought medical attention.

Sheriff Passmore went to McDonald's farm the next day, a Sunday, and arrested him. McDonald posted bond and was released from jail.

At that point, two men wanted Carter dead.

McDonald later paid a fine and was warned to stay away from Carter, and Carter was told once again to keep his farm animals on his own property.

Meanwhile, Joe Rawlins launched an intense lobbying effort against Carter during the winter months of 1904-05. Once the crops were harvested and rural folks had a chance to visit, Joe told neighbors and townspeople alike that all he wanted was peace and that Carter would not let him be.

"I'm sick and tired of bein' hauled into court every time I turn around," he told a group in Webb's Mercantile store in Hahira one December day. "If Carter keeps lyin' 'bout me and my family, I may have to kill him. And if I do, y'all know that he deserves it. This thing has got to the point that I don't believe that killing him would be a sin in the eyes of God. So, if you got any sway with him at all, tell him to back off. Better yet, tell him that I'll buy his property if he'll move out of the county and stay away from me and my family for good."

When Carter heard about that proposition the following Saturday, he scoffed and said, "To hell with Rawlins. I'll buy him out. Tell him that." He started to leave the store, but then turned to the gathering of a dozen men and said, "The only reason you brought that up is because y'all are on Rawlins' side. All of you can go to hell."

There was little doubt that public sentiment ran strongly in Rawlins' favor. People he hardly knew would hail him and ask how things were going. Usually, Joe would just say that everything was going to be all right and leave it at that. At other times, he railed against Carter and said he would surely have to kill him one day.

6

AS SPRING PLANTING BEGAN, JOE BECAME MORE AND MORE agitated with Carter. Every time they met on the road or in town, harsh words were exchanged. Neither showed any sign of backing away from an inevitable showdown.

Angeline could hardly talk to Joe without the conversation turning to Carter, and Joe's temper would flare. Worry and dread settled over Angeline. People often asked her why she didn't urge her husband to make peace. Angeline would shake her head and say that she was doing all she could to head off trouble.

In late March, Carter's mule got into Joe's recently planted crops and bit off hundreds of sprouts. Joe shot the mule dead on the spot, then tied a rope to its hind legs and, using his plow horse, dragged the carcass onto Carter's property.

When a deputy sheriff showed up with a warrant, Joe went into town and posted bond. When he returned home, he was in a murderous mood. He took down the pistol that Angeline had coaxed him to stop carrying, and he set out to look for Carter. But Carter had gone to Valdosta and wouldn't be back until the next day. His absence gave Joe just enough time to cool off.

Instead of seeking out Carter the next day, Joe appeared calm and confident. He'd decided to play the waiting game. If he ever caught Carter trespassing again, he told several of his friends, then he could solve his legal problems with a load of buckshot and not have to worry about the consequences.

"If I don't do somethin', he'll break me in court, make me spend all of my money on bonds and lawyers," he said.

Meanwhile, news of the escalating trouble between Rawlins and Carter reached Squire Jowers, and he dispatched his son, Gene, with a message.

Gene rode up to the Rawlins place one spring afternoon and, after a warm welcome, everyone gathered around the dining room table as Gene ate and told them all of the news from Coffee County.

Finally, Gene's face turned serious and he said, "Pa sent me over here. He says this thing between you and Carter has gone on long enough. He wants you to sell out and move back to Coffee County."

For a moment, Joe sat there with a stunned expression on his face. Then he launched into a tirade of cursing like none in the room ever had heard before.

"Sell out? Hell, no. I've worked too hard. I've worked too God-damned hard. We're just finishing up this new house. Ain't even got the chimney built yet. We've made a lot of friends in eight years. No, hell, no! We're not going to turn tail to Carter and leave."

He stormed out of the house and didn't return until well after dark. Gene was asleep when he came into the house, but a worried Angeline was sitting up.

"Pa is just concerned about us, Joe," she said. "He wants us to be happy and live without all this trouble."

Joe just nodded and went to bed without uttering a word.

Next morning, Gene saddled his horse and led it to the front of the house. Joe and Angeline stood on the porch.

"What do you want me to tell Pa? Want us to bring the wagons?" he asked hopefully.

Quickly, Angeline interjected, "Joe, maybe we ought to –"

"No, damn it," Joe said as he turned angrily on his wife. He gave her a hard look and then turned back to Gene. "Tell

Squire we're staying here. Tell him Carter don't have long to live. He's a dead man and don't even know it."

Joe heard Angeline gasp as she turned and went into the house.

"Tell him we're staying," Joe said again, and then he, too, went inside.

A STRANGE PEACEFULNESS SETTLED OVER THAT REGION FOR A couple of months. As neighbors of Carter and Rawlins awaited a showdown, nothing happened. When court was held at the little courthouse on Val Del Road, Rawlins received no notice to appear and he decided to let matters rest while he cultivated his crops.

But Carter didn't let it rest. He went to Valdosta and complained to the superior court judge that his case had been pushed aside by a magistrate who was friends with Rawlins. When Joe heard about Carter's complaint, his blood began to boil again.

Before Rawlins could make a court appearance, Carter was back in Valdosta, taking out another warrant, this one charging Milton with highway robbery. He claimed that Milton took some money from his son Willie. Milton denied it but Carter went before a grand jury and got an indictment against Milton.

A few days after the indictment, Milton saw Carter working in a field about a hundred yards from his house. By that time, male members of the Rawlins family were known to keep guns close at hand. Milton grabbed a shotgun from the bed of the wagon and went after Carter, threatening to kill him as Carter sprinted the short distance to his house.

Milton, Carter would later testify, came into his home, still threatening him with the shotgun, and Ella Carter, W.L. Carter's wife, coolly intervened. She told Milton to get out of her house and asked if he was going to shoot a woman. Milton left.

When Joe Rawlins heard about the incident, he told Tim McDonald that it was only a matter of time until he solved all of his problems with Carter with a load of buckshot. He waited only a couple of days to try to make good on that threat.

Joe was hunting stray calves in the woods at the back of his property, and it happened that he was carrying a shotgun. When he saw Carter in the woods, he dropped into a ditch, aimed the shotgun and fired at the other man. He believed that he had killed his long-time enemy.

Joe went immediately to the home of William E. Martin, a highly respected farmer who had tried to remain friends with both men and lived only a couple of hundred yards from the Rawlinses. He told Martin that he had run upon Carter on his land and Carter had taken a shot at him. Rawlins said he returned fire and killed Carter.

Word spread like wildfire in the community and a number of curious people ran toward the woods to view the dead man. Instead of a dead man, they found Carter very much alive. Although seriously wounded in the left side and hip, he was dragging himself toward his home. As a crowd gathered, Ella Carter arrived at the scene to help her husband to their house several hundred yards away.

But, before leaving the scene, Carter swore he had no weapon and that Rawlins had ambushed an unarmed man. The bystanders launched a thorough search of the area but found no weapon. Some immediately questioned Rawlins' character for shooting what certainly appeared to be an unarmed man.

In his defense, Joe said someone must have taken the gun and hid it, but he could not explain why anyone would have done Carter a favor by taking the gun away and leaving him to possibly die alone in the woods from a gaping wound in his side.

Sheriff Passmore rode out to the Rawlins farm the next day and questioned Joe about the shooting. Joe said he definitely saw a gun in Carter's hands and that Carter was raising it to fire, but Joe fired first. The sheriff seemed satisfied with Joe's version, and he left without arresting Rawlins.

But others soon informed the sheriff that no gun had been found. The sheriff said he would take up the matter again as soon as Carter was able to talk to him, and at the moment Carter was in no shape to talk.

Carter told several people who visited him during his recovery period that he planned to take out a peace warrant against Rawlins as soon as he was well enough to make a trip to Valdosta. When Rawlins heard about it, he made no secret that a peace warrant would only heighten hostilities.

S. S. Kemp, a Methodist preacher from Hahira who had tried for months to defuse the situation, talked with Carter and then carried a message of peace to Rawlins. "Mr. Carter says he is willing to become friends with you and never mention your name again except in kindness," the preacher told Rawlins.

However, Joe told the preacher that it was too late for forgiveness, that his grievance was great and he felt only the need for vengeance. It was simply too late to make peace, he said.

Then Joe added, "By the way, preacher, I understand that Carter will put me under a peace bond. If he does, it will disarm me as far as acting in the open is concerned, but I will kill him if I have to crawl on my stomach to his place, lay around it all night and shoot him through the cracks as he sits by his fireplace. A peace warrant will force me to act in the dark."

Sure enough, Carter swore out a peace warrant, and on Saturday, June 10, 1905, Rawlins and two bondsmen signed a $1,200 peace bond. As soon as the bond was signed, Rawlins flew into another rage and cursed Carter openly. He said he wanted to take out a peace warrant against Carter, too, but the sheriff was out of town and he was told that he would have to wait until Monday.

Three days later, on a Tuesday afternoon, Rawlins returned to Valdosta, and he seemed to be in a much better mood. He told the sheriff that he was "looking for a permanent solution" to his problems with Carter and that he would hold off on taking a peace warrant. Then he told the sheriff it was so late in the day that he would not be returning to his home that evening, and he took a room at the Daniel Ashley Hotel.

Rawlins made sure people saw him that evening. He sat on the front porch of the hotel late into the night and hailed just about everyone who passed. At one point, he told a small gathering of people, "If old man Carter was killed tonight, I'd get the blame, but you good folks know better. I'm sitting right here in Valdosta talking to you."

All the while, a most vicious crime was being committed. Word about a terrible tragedy near Hahira reached Sheriff Passmore in Valdosta at midmorning on Wednesday. His brother, Dan, called to say that a shootout at W.L. Carter's place had left at least two children dead.

The sheriff shook his head and looked at his long-time chief deputy, J.F. Crosby. "I knew something like this was going to happen," he said. "Nothing but damnable trouble out that way for years. Betcha J.G. Rawlins is mixed up in this."

Crosby nodded in agreement as they headed to the train depot to catch the Shoo-Fly train north. They secured the use of a buggy at the livery stable in Hahira and rode out to the Carter place, a couple of miles east.

The Carter house was overflowing with grieving people. Lora, eldest of the Carter children, was on the porch crying. "They've killed my brother and sister," she sobbed.

Inside, the sheriff viewed the bodies of Willie, age fifteen, and Carrie, age thirteen. Both had died from wounds inflicted by shotgun blasts.

A coroner's jury was formed from among the men present and they were asked to determine the cause of death and identify possible suspects.

W.L. Carter told a harrowing tale to jurors. He said his family had just finished eating the evening meal when a barking dog drew the three oldest children outside. They'd been nursing a sick calf, and the children worried that the dog might be bothering it. The father said he tried to call his children back into the house because of all the trouble he'd been having with the Rawlinses. But only Lora returned immediately.

The father, whose movements were still hampered by wounds from the encounter with Joe Rawlins, said he pulled himself upright at the back door of the main dwelling and called again for Willie and Carrie to come back inside the house. Then he heard his son's rifle fire.

"I hollered, 'What are you doin', Willie?' He said, 'I'm a-shootin', Pa. I see'd a man'."

A moment later, Carter said he saw the muzzle blast from a shotgun beneath a pear tree in the yard, and his son collapsed. Carrie ran to her brother's side and asked, "Buddy, are you hurt?"

At that moment, Carter said, two more blasts came in quick succession from two different guns shrouded by the darkness beneath the tree. Carrie fell to the ground and did not move.

The Carters said they doused the kerosene lamps and barricaded themselves in the house. They called repeatedly to their children but got no response. Then, some four or five minutes after the shots were fired, Willie beat on the front door and called, "Mama, let me in."

They helped Willie into the house and put him on a bed. Although it was dark, Carter said he could feel his son's wounds and he knew the boy would die soon. Willie also was aware of the seriousness of his wounds. "He told his Ma, 'I'm a dead boy, Mama. I cannot live.' I told him, 'Maybe not, son.'

But he said, 'Yes, sir, father, I'm a dead boy. I am shot, and I'm dying'.

"When I asked who shot him, he said, 'Jesse Rawlins shot a load of buckshot through me.' He said Milton Rawlins was standing beside Jesse, and that both fired blasts that killed Carrie. He told his Ma that we didn't need to worry about Carrie. He had checked on her before he came to the house and she was already dead."

As the Carters tried to comfort their son, they heard a noise. The night raiders were trying to stuff corn shucks under the house, Carter told the jurors. The obvious intention was to set it afire.

Lora helped her father pull a board loose that covered a crack in the log house. They peered out. Since it was a moonlit night, they said they could clearly see the figures of the killers.

"The moon was shining bright," Carter said, "and I could see Milton Rawlins maybe ten or twelve feet from the house. Then I saw Jesse with an armload of shucks. Then I saw a Negro."

The elder Carter said he fired a shotgun blast through the crack. "I fired at Jesse, but he jumped back and I heard the sound of running feet. Then Milton Rawlins was saying, 'What in the hell are you running for? Come back here, you God-damn cowards.' And then, a few minutes later, I heard him say, 'If you don't come back and finish the job, I'll see that old man Rawlins don't pay you one damn cent of that hundred dollars he promised you.'

"Then the Negro said, 'I'm a-gonna leave here. This thing is gettin' hot as hell. Y'all better leave, too. That old man is gonna kill somebody.' After that, I didn't hear any more from the Negro."

Carter said the family tried to comfort Willie as he repeatedly asked for a drink of water. "But we couldn't go outside to get the water bucket off the shelf on the front porch," Carter said, his voice cracking with emotion. Through the crack in the wall, they could see Carrie's body, he said, but they were powerless to bring her inside. As the night wore on, the assassins stayed near the house. Willie died just after sunup, Carter said, and the killers left shortly afterward. The Carters began to holler for neighbors to come to their aid.

His story finished, Carter told the sheriff, "You can go get the Rawlins boys." He also asked the sheriff to look for the black man who had come by his place earlier in the day.

The coroner's jury agreed that the Rawlins boys ought to be arrested.

Neighbors who had arrived at the crime scene hours ahead of the sheriff pointed out tracks between the Rawlins house and the Carter house—four sets coming toward the Carter home and only three sets leading away. Some of the footprints, made in freshly plowed ground, were unique. A pair of brogans with one heel missing and nails sticking out left distinctive marks.

The lawmen loaded into the buggy and drove to the Rawlins house. They approached the house with guns drawn and later said the Rawlins boys seemed surprised when advised they were under arrest. They flatly denied having been to the Carter place during the night and said they had not heard any gunshots.

Their mother said the boys had been at home all night after plowing all day on Tuesday. Joe Rawlins was not at home, Angeline said. He'd spent the night in Valdosta. The sheriff handcuffed all three boys without resistance and put them in the buggy. The boys' sisters broke into uncontrollable sobbing as the boys were hauled away to the Carter house and the scene of the crime.

IN VALDOSTA, JOE RAWLINS WAS PICKING UP LEGAL PAPERS AT the office of his attorneys when he heard about the shootings.

Dan Passmore had called, Rawlins was told, and said two Carter children had been killed.

"I hope that's not true," Rawlins told several people gathered at the legal office. "I hope it is a false alarm. I can't believe anyone would do something like that. Kill children? That's awful. That's an unforgivable sin in the eyes of God."

On the street, Joe met Bob Thomas, brother of Solicitor General Will Thomas. "They are going to have you arrested here directly, Joe," Thomas said.

"They can have me arrested if they want to," Rawlins said. "I haven't done anything to be arrested. I've been here since yesterday afternoon."

Thomas said, "I thought you might want to go home and take care of your business before they arrest you."

"I'm not going to turn tail and run," Rawlins replied. "Sure, I hate Carter, but I've been in town all night. They can arrest me if they want to, but I ain't done nothin' to deserve it."

A short time later, a deputy sheriff arrested Joe Rawlins on the street and took him to the jail. The sheriff had not previously required Joe to post a bond on the assault charge. However, before leaving for Hahira, the sheriff told his deputies that if Rawlins could be found, they should lock him up until he had a chance to sort out the events near Hahira.

In less than two hours, Rawlins managed to get a bondsman to sign his bail, and he was on the street again. He went directly to the livery stable and hired a hackman to drive him to the north end of the county. A mile from his house, he told the driver he would walk the rest of the way. "Maybe I'll meet my boys between here and home," Joe said.

But he didn't meet his boys. When he reached his house, he found it was empty. As he started toward the old house about three hundred yards away to see if anyone was there, he saw Deputy Crosby and another lawman coming toward the new house. Crosby hailed Joe and told him to come to the road so they could talk.

"What are you doing here?" Crosby asked. "Did you make bond?"

"Sure did," Rawlins answered.

"Well, I gotta re-arrest you. Get in the buggy."

"What's going on now?" Joe asked. "Why am I being arrested?"

"It's in connection with the shootings at the Carter house," the deputy said. "I came over here to look at your guns. Let's go to the house. I want to see them now."

As the two men walked inside, Joe asked, "What evidence have you got that my boys had anything to do with the killings?"

"Pine-blank evidence," the deputy answered, using a common South Georgia corruption of the term point-blank. "The Carters say your boys were there and tracks from there to here correspond. Now the coroner's jury wants to see any guns you've got."

Joe brought out two shotguns. The deputy broke open the first one, smelled the chamber and determined that it had not been fired recently. The other one was rusty and obviously had not been fired in years.

"That one is all cancered up," Joe said. It required the efforts of both men to finally break it open. "See, the shell in there is all cancered up, too."

The deputy put both guns aside, but Joe was adamant about the coroner's jury viewing the guns. "Those are my guns. I want the coroner's jury to see them. Let's take them with us."

"No need," Crosby said. "I'll tell them what I found here."

The deputy put Joe in the buggy without handcuffs and drove to the Carter house. Sheriff Passmore came outside and talked with the deputy. They decided to release Joe since he had made bond on the assault charge.

"Just don't think about taking any trips," the sheriff warned. "If you run, we'll find you."

"I ain't goin' anywhere," Joe said. "I ain't got no reason to run. And I don't think my boys have, either. This is a mistake. I'll bet someone was trying to rob old man Carter. He keeps a lot of money around the house, I've heard."

The sheriff started to walk away, but Joe called to him. "Listen, sheriff, if my boys are accused of something this bad, I'm afraid someone might try to kill them or lynch them. Can I hire a guard to make sure they're safe?"

"They'll be OK, Mr. Rawlins. You go on home and take care of your business."

Joe made no effort to leave. When the sheriff noticed, he walked back to Joe and said, "Stay away from the boys. They're in custody, and no one talks to them between here and the jail."

Joe stayed where they could see him, hoping his presence might boost their morale. When the sheriff and his party finally left for the train station, Joe jumped into a neighbor's buggy and followed the procession to Hahira. He didn't have a chance to talk to the boys there, either. But they didn't appear to be worried, and he was happy about that.

Joe saw someone he recognized standing near his boys—Frank Turner, a black bricklayer who had been working on a brick chimney at the new Rawlins house. Joe approached him and said, "Where have you been, Frank? You ain't been workin' the past couple of days. Is that chimney ever gonna get finished?"

As he spoke, Turner turned toward him and Joe saw the handcuffs. Before Turner could reply, Deputy Crosby said, "Just shut up and move along, Mr. Rawlins. You ain't talking to this man. He's under arrest, too. And you need to keep your distance unless you want to go with us."

Joe shook his head and walked away. Then he saw Joe Bentley, one of Turner's closest friends, standing nearby and he asked, "Why do they have Frank?"

"They got him suspicioned as being mixed up in the killings. I told him that white people's business was for white people and niggers' business was for niggers. But he wouldn't never listen. Now he's messed around and got hisself in a peck of trouble."

"Well, I'll be damned," Joe said. "He's under suspicion, too?"

As the lawmen and prisoners boarded the train for Valdosta, Joe got in the borrowed buggy and headed eastward toward his home. It was past dark when Joe arrived at home, and he found a very upset Angeline waiting for him.

"What are we going to do?" she wailed. "They've locked up the boys. We've got to do something. My God, I can't believe this is happening." And she burst into tears—again. Joe had noticed before the outburst that her eyes were red and puffy and her cheeks were raw, like a wintertime chap. She'd obviously done a lot of crying in the past few hours. Joe pulled her close to him and tried to comfort her. "We'll go to town in the morning and bond them out," he said. "We can work this thing out. We'll be all right."

Angeline looked directly into her husband's eyes and said, "What have you done. Joe? Did you get the boys mixed up in this?"

Joe turned away from her without speaking and went to bed. It had been a very long day, and he was asleep within minutes.

Angeline was alone with her thoughts and her suspicions. The girls were staying at the McDonalds' house for the night, and Angeline was left alone to wrestle with her disturbing thoughts and suspicions. She decided her boys would not want to eat jail food, so she started cooking and baking. Like always, she wanted to do the best she could for them.

But she could not escape a terrible feeling that her family was about to be torn apart, and she felt helpless to do anything about it. With that thought, more tears flowed through the night.

Joe knew his boys were going to need a lawyer, and a very good one, too. All lawyers wanted money up front, and good lawyers wanted a lot of it. Joe had the money he'd borrowed at the bank, but he already had plans for that. So he chose another way to raise money quickly. Watermelons were in, so Joe got up before daylight, rousted out a couple of hired hands and put them to loading the wagon with the biggest and tastiest watermelons in his fields. He would sell the load for whatever it would bring at the farmer's market in Valdosta and use the money to hire a lawyer or post bond for the boys.

Angeline filled a picnic basket with the food she had cooked and put it in the wagon. After the long and sleepless night, her eyes were red and her face was drawn. She felt like the world was falling in on her.

On the way to town, Joe stopped the wagon at the McDonald house so they could reassure the girls that everything was going to be all right. Before they left, Joe took Tim McDonald aside and told him that he needed money for legal fees and bond. McDonald owed him forty dollars, but he came up with only ten. Joe stuck that money in his pocket. He had high hopes for a big payoff on the watermelons

In Valdosta, Joe tethered the team near the jail and went inside to make sure he and Angeline could see the boys. But a surprise awaited him. As he walked into the sheriff's office, he found four stern-faced men—the sheriff, two deputies, and a jailer holding a shotgun aimed at him.

Sheriff Passmore said, "OK, Mr. Rawlins, just raise your hands where we can see them."

"What's going on?" Joe asked.

"You're under arrest."

"I made my bond yesterday."

"This time, it's accessory to murder, Mr. Rawlins."

Joe wore a stunned expression as he was searched and placed in a cell.

7

ALTHOUGH IT WAS THURSDAY, THE CROWD THAT JAMMED Valdosta's downtown streets was larger than any Saturday gathering. Two factors focused public interest on the Carter case. First, the murder victims were children, and few crimes stirred more emotion than the killing of children. Second, people who had heard about the long-running feud between Rawlins and Carter were hungry for details.

The Valdosta paper, a twice-weekly publication, simply could not satisfy the demand for information. Newsletters were posted on a bulletin board outside the newspaper's offices on days when the paper was not published. But the newsletters never seemed to be up to date. Talk on the street stayed one step ahead of the reported items, as fact became gossip and gossip became fact. At times, the general public did not seem to care which was which.

As a festival atmosphere took over the mood of the town, every train that screeched to a stop at the depot brought more people asking the same questions over again. Reporters for daily newspapers in Macon, Atlanta, Savannah, and Jacksonville, Fla., arrived and began assembling the shocking details. The case quickly became front-page news in every city in Georgia.

C. C. Brantley, editor of the *Valdosta Times*, and his staff could not keep up with queries from newspapers that did not dispatch a reporter to the scene, and, at one time, Brantley ordered that the telephone not be answered until Saturday's edition was on the streets.

"We had enough news to fill up the pages two or three times," he explained later. "We did not need the constant telephone calls. They weren't doing our paper any good. The callers were seeking information, not offering it. We resembled an information booth at a busy train station."

All telegraph and telephone lines running into Valdosta were jammed with inquiries. Reporters tried to run down every rumor, but they were soon swamped with the true and untrue. A reporter for a New York newspaper said he'd heard before his arrival in Valdosta that an entire family of twelve had been wiped out by nightriders. But only nine members of the Carter family were in the house that night—the parents and seven of their nine children. Valdosta, previously a quiet farming community in South Georgia, was suddenly on everyone's map.

INSIDE THE JAIL, JOE RAWLINS RANTED ALMOST CONSTANTLY from his arrest on Thursday until legal help arrived on Saturday. Sometimes, he was loud, demanding, and profane in his quest for legal assistance. Summer's heat was just beginning, and most outer doors and windows were left standing open. People on the street could hear parts of his shouted pleas.

"Hey, someone send me a lawyer," he hollered. "I'm locked up and I ain't got a lawyer. I've got money. I can pay. Send me a lawyer."

When his demands failed to produce a lawyer, he would curse all lawyers for being "gutless and afraid" of public sentiment. Or he would engage in self-pity, yelling out, "I don't understand why my friends won't help me out of this fix."

Rawlins became particularly upset when a copy of the
June 15 edition of the *Macon Telegraph* was passed to him. His
face reddened as he read, "Rawlings (sic) was in the city
yesterday and spent the night here, so it will be easy for him
to prove that he did not do the shooting, although, on account
of the feud, people are quick to connect his name with it. It
has been predicted all along that there would be bloodshed in
that community, but no one dreamed it would be two young
and inoffensive people to suffer. The Carter home has been
thronged with people today (Thursday), and people who
were disposed to lay much of the blame for the feud on
Carter now deeply sympathize with him."

The article also said that "people in that community are in
a frame of mind to measure swift punishment upon the guilty
parties, or the instigators."

Rawlins hollered, "Tell that damned reporter from Macon
that I wanna see him. Tell him to come to the jail and face me.
I want to know if he is tryin' to get all of us lynched." The
reporter already had returned to Macon by train earlier in the
day.

On Friday, Squire Jowers came to town. First, he talked to
Angeline, who had been trying to secure a lawyer without
success. Then he paid a visit to the jail and talked to his son-
in-law and grandsons. All four vehemently denied any
involvement in the killings, and Jowers began hunting a
lawyer. He talked to several in Valdosta, but none was
willing to take on the highly charged case.

T. H. Noland, a young attorney who had been in practice
in Valdosta less than a year, would later testify in a change of
venue hearing that he met with Jowers and considered taking
the case. But as soon as Jowers' visit became public
knowledge, Noland said more than a dozen influential people
"told me not to have anything to do with that case."

Meanwhile, one name kept cropping up. Jowers was told
that John Randolph Cooper of Macon was well known in
Valdosta for getting favorable verdicts in Lowndes County

courts. He would take cases that other lawyers refused, but his services did not come cheaply. His reputation and name recognition, not to mention his courtroom tenacity and unusual legal expertise, put him in the highest of pay brackets.

But Jowers could afford it. He called Cooper, and the attorney arrived in Valdosta on Saturday. By that time, Joe Rawlins' fits had become the talk of the town. And one thing that pushed Rawlins into such a rage was a jailhouse rumor that Alf Moore, a black laborer whom he had met a year or more before, was booked into the jail just before noon and had made a confession that implicated Joe Rawlins and his sons.

Rawlins, who shared a cell with Milton, knew that Joe Bentley had been arrested after they had met in Hahira on Wednesday. And, of course, Rawlins knew that Frank Turner was in jail. But, with the arrival of Moore, Rawlins became even more vocal. People on the street could hear him shouting, "Hey, sheriff, how many niggers does it take to convict a white man in Lowndes County?"

Rawlins also bickered constantly about not being able to talk to his two younger sons, Leonard and Jesse, who were placed together in a cell in a different part of the jail. But, every now and then, Joe would holler, "Hey, Jesse. Hey, Leonard. I'm taking care of things. We'll have a lawyer in here shortly. Meantime, don't tell anyone a damned thing. They ain't got no right to question you. Tell 'em to go to hell."

On Friday evening, Rawlins secured the help of a jail trustee to check on his boys and make sure they had gotten his message.

With Cooper's arrival on Saturday, Rawlins settled down considerably. Although Cooper seldom smiled and did not engage in idle talk, he exuded confidence and that was something Joe Rawlins desperately needed.

He immediately implored Cooper to find out what the two black men who'd been arrested—Joe Bentley and Frank

Turner—might have told investigators. What Cooper learned was not what Rawlins wanted to hear. Although the sheriff told Cooper that no one had confessed any part in the crime, rumors persisted that Alf Moore had also been arrested and was cooperating with investigators.

If anyone doubted the rumor, the truth came to light when the *Macon Telegraph* hit the streets of Valdosta on Sunday morning. "Chain tightens about Rawlings (sic)," the headline read. Joe Rawlins' face whitened as he read, "Alf Moore...a Negro alleged to be connected with the killing of the Carter children...told a startling story after his arrest. He declares that he was employed by Rawlings (sic) to aid in the bloody work.

"He says that before leaving for Valdosta the day the children were killed, Rawlings (sic) carried his supper to him in the woods in order to keep him from going home. He also said the program was to kill the whole family and burn the house. He says Milton Rawlings (sic) shot Carrie and Jesse Rawlings (sic) killed Willie Carter.

"The gun with which one of them was killed also was found today. Excitement over the disclosure is high and heavy guards will remain at the jail tonight."

When Rawlins finished reading the dispatch, he stood up and grabbed the bars of the cell door. Clanking the door as loudly as he could, Rawlins began shouting obscenities and proclaiming the innocence of himself and his boys. He also hollered for the public to direct the Macon reporter to his cell because "he's talking to a lyin' bastard and he could get us lynched by puttin' that kind of trash in the paper." This time, not even Cooper could talk Rawlins into quieting down. Finally, the attorney shook his head in disgust and left the jail.

On Monday, Cooper persuaded Oscar M. Smith, a Valdosta lawyer, to team up with him. And with that sort of buffer, even Noland let it be known that he was available. But Cooper deemed Smith's services adequate to "ferret out witnesses and get the lay of the land when it comes time to select jurors."

During the next few days, both sides laid plans for the coming trials. Solicitor General Will Thomas made no secret of his intention to try the Rawlins boys first. He needed convictions against them to have any case at all against Joe Rawlins, since the father was charged only as an accessory.

Meanwhile, Squire Jowers, the former Coffee County sheriff, was establishing a close rapport with Sheriff Passmore, and Passmore revealed details about the case to Jowers that he might not have shared with anyone else. Passmore was convinced that Joe had commanded his sons to take part in the raid on the Carter house, and the more the two men talked, the more Jowers became convinced that Joe had instigated the whole affair.

When Jowers confronted his son-in-law and told him that the evidence was overwhelmingly against him, Joe flatly denied any involvement and was indignant that his father-in-law might question his professed innocence. He told Jowers that he was in Valdosta that night and did not believe his boys were involved, either. That, of course, was what Jowers wanted to hear, even though the sheriff was equally adamant that all of the evidence pointed to the guilt of the boys and their father.

The *Valdosta Times* sent a reporter to the jail every day — and sometimes more than once — to gather information for its Wednesday and Saturday editions. But even with that, editor Brantley felt smothered by the reports in out-of-town newspapers, and the possibility of becoming a daily publication was frequently discussed.

Just when Moore's confession was hogging the headlines, the case took on historic importance. If the Rawlins trials were held during the county's regular term of superior court in August, the entire session would be consumed by those trials alone. So Judge Robert Mitchell decided to set a precedent. He ordered the first special term of court ever held in the county to dispose of the Carter murder cases. The first trial would begin on July 17, he said.

As soon as that date was set, attorney Cooper convened a strategy session for the defense. He secured the sheriff's permission to gather all four Rawlinses in one cell for a while, and with attorney Smith at his side, they went over the charges, scrutinized the list of state's witnesses and compiled a witness list of their own.

Cooper said he could find only three areas of state's evidence that could be worth contesting—testimony by the Carters, testimony by one or all of the black men being held, and the physical evidence gathered by investigators.

"It should not be difficult to impeach the Carters' testimony," he said. "This feud has been simmering for twenty years. The jury will take anything they say with a grain of salt. We will question their ability to identify people by moonlight, and downplay the boy's dying statement as hearsay.

"But we want to go one step farther with W.L. Carter. We want to subpoena as many witnesses as possible who will testify that they have had problems with Carter. We will sow doubt in the jurors' minds about whether someone else might have tried to kill Carter that night for the cotton money he flashed around Hahira. And we want witnesses who will testify about Carter's character, that he is a liar and cannot be believed even under oath in a courtroom. By impeaching his testimony, we also will be impeaching the testimony of his wife and daughter."

The defense team started a list of potential witnesses that day which would eventually include sixty names. Subpoenas issued by the state would run the witness list to more than a hundred, making it potentially the most cumbersome trial in the history of Lowndes County. Hardly half that many people ever had been summoned to a trial in the county before.

Cooper's second area of concern was possible testimony by Joe Bentley, Frank Turner and Alf Moore.

"Once again, we will impeach any testimony," he said, "and that should not be too difficult. Negroes don't make very good witnesses. Most of them are easily confused, and we should be able to get them to backtrack on almost anything they say."

He seemed satisfied that he could handle those matters, and he added, "Without corroborating testimony, the physical evidence means virtually nothing. We'll sow doubt about any guns that can be connected to the defendants by saying they were stolen. As far as those tracks across the fields are concerned, the state will have the burden to prove whether they were made at nine o'clock at night or nine o'clock in the morning."

When the meeting concluded, Joe Rawlins suddenly stood up, enthusiastically shook Cooper's hand and said, "I was told you were the best attorney in Georgia. By God, now I believe it."

Cooper was not moved by the compliment. He surveyed all of the defendants and said, almost coldly, "You've got to keep a lid on things. Don't talk to anyone about any aspect of this case without first talking to Mr. Smith or me. I won't be in town every day, but he will, and he can reach me by telephone any time he wants."

After he stepped outside the cell, he turned to Joe and said, "Try to act like a innocent man and stop all this hollering and cussing. You aren't accomplishing a thing with that kind of conduct. Can you do that?"

Joe hung his head down as Cooper finished speaking, nodded and sat down on his cot, never looking up.

Just when Cooper felt like he had some control over the fiery Joe Rawlins, he nearly lost his own cool. On a Tuesday, the day before the *Valdosta Times* would hit the streets, the *Macon Telegraph* reported that Alf Moore's confession "was made public."

The story contained details obviously intended to prejudice the case.

Moore says the elder Rawlings (sic) employed him and that he and the Rawlingses (sic) went to the Carter house. They were to kill the father and mother and the oldest son, set fire to the house and kill the children as they ran out.

The boy came out at the sound of the barking dog and one of the Rawlings (sic) boys shot him. Carrie Carter started toward him, saying 'Buddy, are you hurt?' and she, too, was shot.

Moore said he ran away just as one of the Rawlings (sic) boys was about to set fire to the house to drive its occupants out.

After reading the story while standing on the street, Cooper went directly to Judge Mitchell's office to register a complaint about the tactics of the prosecution. Of course, nothing could undo the damage that had been done, but the judge called the prosecutors and the sheriff together and warned against giving out such information to the press.

From the time of that meeting until the court session began, few new details appeared in any of the papers.

On July 12, the *Macon Telegraph* caused a stir with this report:

Mum has been the words with the Rawlingses (sic). But a day or so ago, some of the officials tried to pump Jesse, youngest of the Rawlings (sic) boys. He was taken to a room in the lower part of the jail and a determined effort was made to make him say something.

He finally told his questioners, "I know what you are thinking; you are wondering what I am thinking," and he said it with the air of one who delighted in having the other side guessing. "Well, how do you feel with these charges hanging over you?" he was asked.

"I don't know," was his quick reply. "I have not thought about it enough to tell."

Of course, Cooper registered another strong complaint with Judge Mitchell. The judge said investigators had the right to question a suspect, but the officials had erred in not allowing Jesse to have his attorney present and he warned against any further infractions.

On the day before the first trial, both sides announced that they were ready to try what was billed as the most publicized murder trial in the history of South Georgia.

8

THE DAY DAWNED HOT AND MUGGY, BUT THAT DID NOT DETER a record crowd from gathering in downtown Valdosta for the beginning of the Rawlins trials. By the time Judge Robert Mitchell entered the courtroom promptly at ten o'clock on that Monday morning, the temperature outside was approaching the ninety-degree mark. Weather buffs predicted a hundred degrees would be reached by mid-afternoon.

Although the new Lowndes County courthouse—which had been completed in the spring—was equipped with the latest in electric fans, those contraptions simply moved the humid air around.

The Carter case was the first to be tried in the new courtroom with its sweeping curved banisters of polished oak that separated officials from the general public. A more memorable case could hardly have been chosen to christen the new building.

A throng of people, estimated at "several thousand" by the *Valdosta Times*, stretched the capacity of hotels and restaurants in the city. The two largest hotels, the Daniel Ashley and the Florence, were filled to capacity by Sunday afternoon, and restaurants were contracting with local farmers to bring enough food to feed the masses. Some ambitious business owners, like J. J. McCranie, owner of the town's largest restaurant, saw the crunch coming. He had lined up dozens of town residents who were willing to rent rooms for a night or for the whole week.

As a couple of thousand people milled on the streets and sought refuge from the heat in shady spots around the courthouse square, hundreds more jammed the hallways. Deputies and bailiffs tried to keep a passage open through the doors and hallways, but it was a constant struggle.

Meanwhile, Sheriff Passmore grappled with problems within the courtroom. Only about 125 spectators could be seated in the courtroom and its balcony, and it was the sheriff's duty to decide who got a seat and who didn't. Besides dealing with the rush of people, the sheriff was dealing with reporters and kinfolk of those involved in the trial.

Judge Mitchell had issued strict orders on how court would be conducted in the new courtroom, and standing was prohibited. That rule put seats at even more of a premium, and the sheriff was left to explain to some of the more influential residents that standing in the aisles or along the walls, a long-time habit in the smaller courtroom in the old courthouse, would not be tolerated.

At ten o'clock, the judge banged his gavel to begin the session. The heat was oppressive as the drama began to unfold. Judge Mitchell noted that, since there was so little crime in Lowndes County, this was the first-ever special session of superior court in the circuit.

Before the defendants could be tried, they would have to be indicted by a grand jury to show that there was cause to hold a trial. Spectators gathered in the hallways and watched with interest as witnesses paraded in and out of the grand jury room to testify. W. L. Carter, Alf Moore, and Deputy Crosby were among those who testified in the closed-door session.

At 1:30, the grand jury returned murder indictments against Milton, Leonard, and Jesse Rawlins and Alf Moore. Joe Rawlins and Frank Turner were indicted as accessories before the fact. The grand jury did not consider charges against Joe Bentley, but he remained in jail. All five of those indicted could face the gallows if convicted.

Less than half an hour later, the Rawlins boys, surrounded by deputies, filed into the courtroom to hear the indictments against them. Each was dressed in a gray suit and each had a scrubbed-clean look. The *Valdosta Times* reported that the boys "appeared to be in good spirits." They smiled and nodded to their grandfather who, as a former sheriff, was given preferred seating in an area across the room from the trial jury but inside the bar area. The boys also spoke quietly to their mother and sisters who were seated on the first bench beyond the rail closest to the defense table.

As soon as court was called into session and the indictment was read, Cooper rose from his seat and asked the judge for additional time to consult with his clients and witnesses. He said that he had not been accorded the time he believed necessary to prepare for the case, that additional witnesses had been added in the past twenty-four hours, and that he had not been given time to read the indictment. He asked for a continuance until the next day.

Solicitor W. E. Thomas objected to any continuance. After a few moments of consideration, Judge Mitchell, an advocate of speedy trials and swift justice, allowed the defense an hour for extra preparations.

Cooper gathered his witnesses in a room and, at his request, Joe Rawlins was brought from the jail across the street to participate in the consultations. The hour that the judge had allowed the defense stretched into two hours, and the judge finally sent a bailiff to the witness room to remind Cooper of the time.

When Cooper returned to the courtroom, he apologized to the judge for the delay. The judge acknowledged the apology with a curt nod and then issued a stern warning to everyone involved in the case that all sessions would begin promptly at the appointed time and those who delayed the proceedings faced possible contempt charges.

As soon as the judge finished his remarks—and before the trial jury could be brought into the courtroom—Cooper rose to make another motion, this time for a change of venue.

He called three witnesses to support his contention. J. W. Stubbs, the first witness, testified that he did not believe the defendants could get a fair trial in Lowndes County because of the intense feeling among local residents and the high level of pretrial publicity. But, during cross-examination by the solicitor, he relented, saying the intense feeling he'd mentioned was for the crime and not particularly directed at the defendants. He also declined to make an outright statement that his fellow Lowndes countians could not render a fair verdict at that time.

L. L. Webb, the second witness, was also a jury commissioner who qualified people to be jurors. He testified that he did not think the Rawlinses could get a fair trial, but he, too, was soon backed into a corner during cross-examination. He finally admitted that if he didn't think a person would render a fair verdict in each and every case, he would not have approved that person's name to be included in the jury pool.

W. T. Lane testified that the Rawlinses might get a fairer trial if sentiment was allowed to cool for a while. But, under cross-examination, he said the defendants could get as fair a trial in Lowndes County as anywhere else, even with the high emotion that gripped the Hahira district.

None of the three men made the impression on the judge that Cooper had hoped, and then five rebuttal witnesses, all prominent men, said they thought a fair trial could be held in Lowndes County. No one seemed surprised when Judge Mitchell denied a change of venue.

But Cooper was not finished with pretrial motions. He next asked for a continuance because certain witnesses for the defense had not appeared. He called Joe Rawlins to testify, and murmurs rippled across the room as the elder Rawlins made his first appearance in the case. Judge Mitchell banged his gavel to quiet the crowd and then he ordered absolute quiet so witnesses could hear questions and lawyers could hear answers.

Rawlins named six people out of sixty prospective defense witnesses who were not present. Cooper said all six were vital to the defense's effort to impeach Carter's testimony, to testify about his character or to relate problems the witnesses might have had previously with Carter.

Sheriff Passmore was called to testify about whether each of the six witnesses named had been served with subpoenas. He said they had. The judge, obviously determined that the trial would not be stalled, overruled the motion for a continuance but instructed the sheriff to do all in his power to ensure that all witnesses were on hand the following morning.

The attorneys were still sparring over whether separate trials should be held for the boys until Judge Mitchell finally called a merciful end to the first session of court just before seven o'clock.

As the prisoners were led from the courthouse to the jail just across Ashley Street, a huge throng of people who had not been able to get into the courtroom gathered to get a glimpse of the prisoners. Joe Rawlins, feeling good about the first day's proceedings, exchanged greetings with people he knew and even offered a few optimistic words about how the trial would turn out.

A few minutes later, spectators filed out of the courthouse, and a *Macon Telegraph* reporter approached Angeline about an interview. She "gracefully and smilingly declined."

Attorney Cooper, who was walking just behind Angeline, put a hand on her arm and said, "I wish more of your good sense had rubbed off on your husband. If you talk to him tonight, use your influence to keep him in check."

Angeline smiled again and nodded agreement. Although Cooper was tired and wrung out and his clothes were soaked with perspiration, he went to the jail and assured his clients he was doing all he could. He also pointed out that, although all of his motions were rejected, each of those motions would be a point for appeals if they were convicted. The boys' spirits were obviously buoyed by his visit.

Cooper chose not to talk to Joe Rawlins that evening. His most pressing project at the moment was to prepare for tomorrow's session.

Later that evening, Joe asked to see his sons, and the sheriff allowed all of them to gather in Joe's cell. As they approached, the father said, "Leonard, they tell me that you are weakening."

Leonard seemed shocked by the accusation. "I am not," he replied firmly.

"Well, I didn't think you would," his father said.

Whether his father actually had heard such a rumor didn't seem important. If there was a weak link in the family chain, it was Leonard. Joe worried about him more than the other two boys for good reason. He'd never established the same rapport with Leonard that he enjoyed with his other two sons. He never seemed quite like the others. He didn't like hunting and fishing as much as Milton and Jesse and, because of that, Leonard never quite bonded with him like the other two had.

In his early childhood, Leonard sometimes chose to stay around the house, especially when the girls were younger and his mother needed help. He didn't like working in the fields, and he had not been plowing with the other boys the day of the murders. The Carters saw so little of him during the siege that they seemed unsure at times whether he was at the scene. Because of that, Joe feared his son might be in a position to strike a deal to testify against his brothers.

He hoped that wouldn't happen, but he couldn't be sure.

"Be strong," the father said. Then he hugged his son and said, "We're gonna be all right. You've just gotta stay tough and believe that we're gonna be all right."

Then he smiled and added, "How about that lawyer we've got? He's good, ain't he?"

All three of the boys agreed, and they gathered around their father and each of them hugged the old man before returning to their cell. Joe Rawlins felt a little better about Leonard's resolve and stamina. He was glad Leonard was in a cell with the other boys. They were troupers. He had faith in them. Yes, he truly believed they were going to be all right. But one man was not so certain. Squire Jowers, who'd taken a room at the Florence Hotel, was talking to his daughter about the same time Joe was talking to his sons.

"Angeline, tell me what you really know about this."

"I've told you already, Papa," she said. "I heard gunshots that night, and I have my own fears about all this. But neither Joe nor any of the boys have admitted to me that they had a part in it."

"Well, I just finished talking to Sheriff Passmore again, and he said the evidence is so overwhelming that not even John Cooper can get the boys off." He paused a moment, his deep-set eyes staring and his whiskered jaw set in a firm line. "I'm worried, Angeline, really worried. If Joe Rawlins really did what everyone is saying he did—send the boys over there to kill everyone—I wouldn't spend a dime on his defense."

Angeline went to her father and put her arms around him. "I know, Papa. But I don't know what to tell you. As long as Joe maintains his innocence, I'm going to stand by him. I'll sell the farm and livestock if I have to, but I'll stand by him and help all I can with the costs."

Squire Jowers' expression softened and he kissed his daughter's forehead. "You're a good woman. Just like your mama. I'm sorry about the doubts I have. We'll keep going with this until we have some reason not to."

Angeline's arms drew tighter around her father.

9

July 18, 1905

THE SECOND DAY OF THE SPECIAL TERM OF COURT DREW AN even larger crowd than the first. Preliminary sparring by the attorneys was about over, and people who jammed the streets around the courthouse anticipated the long-awaited testimony that was expected to turn rumor into fact.

The *Valdosta Times* was on the streets early and it contained a long account of events leading up to the trial, but nothing on Monday's proceedings. The staff—used to publishing only twice a week—took two to three days to gather material and write the stories needed for an issue. But that Tuesday was different for those seeking up-to-the-minute results. A new publication hit the streets. *The Daily Court Reporter* was a four-page, letter-size newspaper published by Valdosta Printing Company.

Stories in the new publication, obviously not written by professionals, contained many errors. A headline in that first edition proclaimed Milton as Joe Rawlins' second son. He was really the eldest. A story said the Rawlinses were "arranged" in court instead of arraigned. But the modest publication offered the news, and people rushed to buy copies at five cents each, the price of most established newspapers at the time.

No doubt, this competition started the *Times* thinking about going daily. Although there was little time to accomplish that switch during the trials, it was a matter of less than two months before the *Times* became a daily.

Tuesday's session began at 8:00 A.M., assuring moderate temperatures for a couple of hours. However, hundred-degree heat was predicted for mid-afternoon.

Soon after Judge Mitchell opened the session—and before a trial jury could be drawn—attorney Cooper made still another motion. He asked that the indictment be quashed. He argued eight points, any one of which would have voided the indictment, he said. And he backed up his arguments with previous court decisions.

The solicitor said the indictment was valid and cited previous court decisions to support his contention. As soon as the solicitor finished speaking, the judge denied the motion.

The defense then asked for separate trials for the defendants, and the judge agreed. Solicitor Thomas immediately announced that Milton would be tried first. The two younger Rawlins boys were taken from the courtroom, but Joe Rawlins was allowed to sit at the defense table and assist in his son's defense.

As the first panel of prospective jurors was called, a buzz of excitement on the streets below could be heard through the open windows. Only thirty-four prospective jurors were called to choose twelve to try the case. The state used sixteen strikes and the prosecution four. Two were disqualified for cause—W. D. McDonald, brother of Tim McDonald, who had once stabbed Carter during a court proceeding, and W.T. Lane, who had testified in favor of a change of venue.

The last juror was seated by 11:00 A.M.

Wasting no time, the state called twenty-seven witnesses into the courtroom to be sworn. They lined up along the railing, raised their right hands and took the oath. W.L. Carter, his wife Ella and daughter Lora were among those sworn.

Angeline was sitting at the defense table, and just before noon, she asked for her hand satchel, which she said she'd left with a bailiff on the first floor. Sheriff Passmore went to retrieve it and when he returned, he made a startling announcement.

"There's a loaded pistol in this satchel," he said. "I searched it and I found a loaded pistol."

Since the jury was in the room and obviously heard the sheriff's statement, Cooper rose to his feet and made a motion for a mistrial.

The judge ordered the jury out of the courtroom and immediately started a hearing about the pistol. Cooper contended that the sheriff had exhibited "a high excitement" concerning the pistol and his dramatic announcement was sure to prejudice the jury against the defendant. "We cannot get a fair trial with this jury," he concluded.

On cross-examination, Passmore said, "I don't know what authority I had to search the satchel, but I did it because she tried to get that satchel into the jailhouse a couple of times. I've heard from sources that Mrs. Rawlins would try to slip a gun to her husband. She's been to the jail every day since I arrested him, and I think she wanted to get something to him. I would never let her take the satchel inside the jail because I'm satisfied that she wanted to get a pistol to Mr. Rawlins."

Angeline was called to the stand and she testified that she had sent for the satchel to get a letter for the defense attorneys.

"I live ten or twelve miles out in the country," she said. "It's lonely on the road. There's just me and my daughters. One is thirteen and the other is fifteen. We travel alone and we live alone since my husband and sons were arrested. I have the pistol for our protection. I was not trying to slip it to my husband. He says he is innocent and I believe him, so I have no reason for wanting him to escape."

Judge Mitchell overruled the motion for a mistrial and called the jury back into the room. He explained to the jury that Mrs. Rawlins carried the pistol for protection and there was no evidence of a covert motive in having the satchel brought into the courtroom. He instructed jury members to disregard anything they might have seen or heard about the pistol.

The defense's witnesses were then called, but only about half of the sixty that had been subpoenaed were present. Angeline and her daughters were among those sworn, and as soon as they were sworn, the solicitor said Mrs. Rawlins, like all of the other witnesses, should be excluded from courtroom proceedings. Cooper objected but the judge agreed with the prosecution and Angeline left the room.

The judge also told all members of the jury pool to leave the room since they might be drawn in one of the other trials and much of the same evidence would probably be presented in any subsequent trials.

With those rules set, the judge called a recess until two o'clock.

W.L. Carter was the first state's witness. He took the stand immediately after the noon break and, with a sketch of the layout of his farmhouse, outbuildings and fences, he began explaining what happened that fateful evening.

"A little while after dark...the dogs started barking. Willie picked up the rifle, and Carrie and Lora, my oldest daughter, went out there with Willie to see what the dogs were after. We had three little motherless calves out there. I was in the main body of the house and I called, 'Children, come back here.' Lora turned and came back the way she had gone out. When Lora came in, I asked, 'Where is the other children?' and then I heard Carrie say, 'I'm coming.' I heard the rifle shoot. I heard it shoot two or three times, and I said, 'Willie, what are you doing? You're gonna kill them calves.' He said, 'No, Pa, I see'd a man.' I told him again to come back.

"Then a gun fired. I saw where the party was that fired the gun. He was under a peach tree just outside the yard fence. Willie said, 'Oh, Lordy,' and he fell. I heard Carrie say, 'Buddy, are you hurt?' and she started toward him. Two more shots were fired right close together and she fell. I never heard from her anymore."

Carter's voice broke and he sobbed for a few moments before continuing.

"Mrs. Carter started to go out there...." His voice choked again and he paused to compose himself. "Mrs. Carter started out there, but I got hold of her. I told her and Lora to get in the house. I told them to bring me my gun, that they (the attackers) were coming in the house. I saw somebody then. I saw Milton and Jesse Rawlins come through the yard. They come from where the shooting came from. I was standing in the back door when they came by and went around behind the kitchen.

"When they got my gun, I went inside the house and shut all of the doors except the back one. I got back in the dark and waited. Then I saw Willie again. While Milton and Jesse were going around the kitchen, he got up and came to the front door. He knocked and said, 'Mama, let me in.' She opened the door and let him in. We laid him on a bed there in the living room, and he said, 'Mama, I'm a dead boy.' I said, 'Maybe not, son.' He said, 'Yes, sir, father, I'm shot clean through. Jesse Rawlins shot a load of buckshot through me, and I'm dying.' He said we needn't be bothering about Carrie because she was dead."

Attorney Cooper arose at that point and asked that the jury be retired until it could be determined whether Willie's dying declaration about who shot him should be admitted as evidence. The jury left the courtroom and Cooper took up the questioning.

Cooper: "Mr. Carter, were you leading your son to say who shot him? Did you suggest who might have done the shooting?"

Carter: "My son was perfectly rational. I didn't say anything to him to make him say who...shot him. I just asked who shot him. I knew who shot him, but I asked him to see if he was conscious. I didn't tell him I saw who shot him. I never led him at all."

Cooper: "Is it possible that you jumped to a conclusion because of past differences between you and the Rawlinses, and is it possible that you suggested to Willie who shot him?"

Carter: "I didn't make no suggestions. I never made him say anything on account of the feeling I entertain toward the Rawlins boys and their daddy. I didn't jump to no conclusions at all. It was a bright moonlight night, and I saw who did the shooting. I wanted to know if he did."

Judge Mitchell ruled that the testimony was admissible, and the jury returned to the room. With Solicitor Thomas asking questions, the testimony picked up where it left off.

Carter: "It was night, but the moon was shining bright and I wanted to know if my son knew who shot him. He said Jesse Rawlins shot him and Milton shot Carrie. My boy said that on his dying bed...and he repeated it several times during the night. Willie begged us for water, but we didn't go out and get the pail off the shelf on the front porch because Jesse and Milton were standing out there with their guns and we were afraid to try to get water.

"Lora said she wanted to go to Bill Edmondson's house to give the alarm. She didn't go because I looked out a crack in the front door and saw Milton Rawlins standing at the front door with his gun cocked and presented. Then I went to the back door...and I saw Jesse Rawlins at the back door with his gun presented. Then I looked out at the front of the house and I saw a Negro and Leonard Rawlins standing by the gate.

"There was no light in the house. We were afraid the boys would shoot us through the cracks by lamplight. There was another shooting done that night. I shot my breech-loading shotgun one time. It was about one o'clock. I shot because Milton, Leonard, Jesse and the Negro were toting shucks and piling them around the steps. When I saw that, I told my daughter...to pull a piece of plank off a crack in the logs. I stuck my gun through the crack and took sight on Jesse and pulled the trigger. It snapped. I pulled the left-hand trigger and it fired. He (Jesse) made a sudden turn and I missed him.

"I heard them running off, and I heard Milton Rawlins say, 'What the hell are you running for? Come back here, you God-damned cowards.' Then he was talking to someone I couldn't see and he said, 'If you don't come back and finish the job, I will see that old man Rawlins don't pay you one cent of that hundred dollars he promised you.' Then the Negro said, 'I am going to leave. This thing is getting as hot as hell. That old man is gonna kill somebody.' After that, I didn't see the Negro any more.

"The others stayed about the house all night. I saw Jim McDonald one time. That was about one o'clock, long after the killings. Willie died right at sunup. Soon after that, I gave the alarm. I hollered, 'Whooooeeee' and "Murder! Murder!' Tim McDonald nor Jim McDonald—they live only about two hundred and fifty yards away—never came to my house. They didn't go to my children's funeral either.

"Henry McMillan was the first man to reach me. He lived... about a quarter of a mile away. But he was the first to come to my house and find out what the hollering was all about."

After help arrived, Carter said he finally was able to go outside and view Carrie's body. He broke down and cried as he described the condition of her body. "She was shot in the chest and shoulder," he said. "About eighteen buckshot hit her. Her head was stamped in the face...a mashed place in her temple and there were footprints and bruises all over her body. On her arms and legs, you could see the print of tacks in shoes and her head was all buried in the ground."

The spectators gave a collective gasp at these details and several women in the courtroom dabbed tears from their eyes. Milton Rawlins showed no emotion at the revelation, and Joe Rawlins was whispering to defense attorneys.

When Thomas finally said, "No more questions," attorney Cooper began a rigorous hour-and-a-half long cross-examination that was intended to sow doubt in the minds of the jurors.

Cooper bore down on what the defense saw as inconsistencies between Carter's testimony before the coroner's jury and what he had said on the witness stand. Many of the points were covered several times and the solicitor repeatedly objected to the line of questioning, saying the witness already had answered that question or contending that Cooper was badgering the witness.

The defense attorney also pointed out that Carter had not mentioned to the coroner's jury that he had seen Jim McDonald or his father, Tim, near his house the night of the killings. "I didn't say anything about it because I was asked who did the shooting. No one asked me to name everyone I'd seen there. I told them there might have been a dozen men there for all I know."

Carter paused and then added, "'Nother reason I didn't mention them is because Tim McDonald is a brother-in-law to the sheriff, and I was scared right then about what to say. He was investigating. I didn't know what he might do if I said the McDonalds was there."

Another point for cross-examination concerned Carter's ability to make positive identifications by moonlight while peeking through a crack in the wall. Cooper also questioned whether Carter could identify the voices.

"Didn't you testify that your family and the Rawlinses were not on speaking terms, that you ignored them and they ignored you? Hadn't spoken in more than two years? Isn't that what you said? I want to know how you were suddenly able to recognize voices that you seldom, if ever, heard."

Carter repeated much of his earlier testimony and maintained that he recognized the killers by moonlight and recognized their voices.

Cooper then turned to Carter's troubles with other neighbors and alluded to the possibility that any number of people, including the McDonalds, might want Carter dead. Carter admitted to having "a heap of misunderstandings," including several with the McDonalds. "I have prosecuted people in this court...and I have been prosecuted."

He said again that he saw Jim McDonald near his house on the night of the murders.

With Carter becoming increasingly uncomfortable under the relentless questioning, Cooper asked him if he'd had trouble with any black people in that area. Carter said he'd had problems with a few. Cooper then pursued a line of questioning about Carter keeping a lot of cash in his home, that he had flashed it while buying cotton in Hahira and that perhaps his assailants were black men with robbery in mind. Carter tried to discount that theory, saying that "I kept plenty of money around the house, but it was Milton and Jesse Rawlins that shot my children. I'm as positive that I saw them as I am that I'm seeing you right now."

When Cooper finally released the witness, Solicitor Thomas questioned Carter about his relationship with Milton Rawlins. Carter said it was "just as bitter as could be." Cooper objected to the line of questioning, but Thomas said the state proposed to show that a conspiracy existed to exterminate the whole family. The judge allowed Carter to describe his relationship with Milton and recount the incident in which he said Milton chased him into his own house.

With Thomas continuing the questions, he also asked Carter if Alf Moore had come by his house a few hours before the killings and asked for directions to Cat Creek Road. Carter said he didn't know Moore's name at that time, but he had seen Moore being led to and from the jail and that "he was the Negro that came by my house that afternoon."

After more than three hours on the witness stand, Carter was excused at 5:30 P.M.

Alf Moore was called. The town buzzed with excitement. It was his story, his confession of the crime, which people wanted most to hear.

10

July 18-19, 1905

ABSOLUTE STILLNESS GRIPPED THE COURTROOM AS ALF MOORE, a 39-year-old black man of average build, spoke his first words from the witness stand. He smiled as he started testifying.

"My name is Alf Moore. I come from Bristol, Tennessee. I have been in Georgia ten, fifteen years, living up and down this Georgia Southern Railroad, cutting ties from here to Macon and back. I have been living in Coffee County. That's where my wife and children is. I have been at work at Staunton, about a half mile above Lenox in Berrien County. I have been working there about four months, cutting (railroad) ties for Mr. Ivey. I have been in Hahira. I worked there about three years ago.

"I knew where Mr. J.G. Rawlins lived. I cut ties at one time back west of Mr. Rawlins' plantation. I knew Mr. Rawlins. I have been to his house. Bought greens and chickens and eggs from him. I don't remember exactly when we left Hahira. We went from there to Abbeville on the Ocmulgee River to cut ties.

"I went to Hahira again the tenth day of June, 1905. I had a talk with Frank Turner. I stayed in Hahira that night, left Hahira Sunday night on the Shoo-Fly (train) and went to Valdosta. I went back to Hahira on Tuesday morning. I sits around there for a while...and then I puts my foot in the road and walks out to J.G. Rawlins' place.

"I met Mr. Rawlins between the house he is living in now and the old house. He said, 'Howdy, Alf.' I said, 'Howdy.' Then he took me to a little shanty in Mr. Rawlins' field and we talks. He tells me, 'Nigger, I will give you a hundred dollars to kill Mr. Carter and Mrs. Carter, and to kill the oldest girl and the oldest boy, I will give you a thirty-two (caliber) pistol.'"

When Moore said that, Cooper rose to his feet and objected, saying that the confession on which the testimony was based was not freely and voluntarily given. Attorneys argued the point for several minutes and each cited Supreme Court decisions concerning confessions. The judge overruled the objection and Moore's testimony continued.

Cooper rose again and tried to continue. Newspaper accounts described his argument as "vehement" against the admission of Moore's confession, and the aggressive nature of the defense attorney's argument signified the importance of his testimony. The *Times* described the scene: "As attorney Cooper warmed up, he pounded the desk (table) in front of him as Milton Rawlins sat with a fan up to his face to conceal the smile which the vehemence of his attorney evoked."

The judge finally told Cooper in a tone of finality that he already had ruled on that point and the testimony would be allowed.

Cooper, his face dripping with perspiration in the heat of the courtroom, stood for a few more seconds, almost defiantly, before finally taking a seat. The solicitor directed Moore to continue his testimony.

Moore: "Mr. Rawlins said, 'I had rather do this myself, but I have already shot him and he got me under a twelve hundred dollar peace bond and he got a bill against me for shooting him and he got me accused of stealing twelve head of hogs. If I don't do away with him, he will break me.'

Cooper said loudly, "Objection! This testimony is a continuation of a confession that was not freely and voluntarily given by the witness. The defense objects—"

The judge's gavel hit the bench and Judge Mitchell said sternly, "I have ruled on that already, Mr. Cooper. Now sit down!"

Cooper slowly sank into his chair and let his head droop almost to the table.

The judge told Moore to continue.

Moore: "Then he told me to stay there and he left. He come back about one o'clock and brought a gun, a zinc bucket with a frying pan turned upside down over it and a watermelon in a croaker sack. In the bucket . . . (there were) some greens and roasting ears in it, and some bread and meat. I eats dinner, and Mr. Rawlins sits there and talks to me. He stayed with me a right smart while...and I ate.

"Near about two o'clock, I seen three more gentlemen. They rapped on the door and Mr. Rawlins opened it. They walked in—Milton, Leonard and Jesse. Then he gave us our charges. Without calling my name, he said, 'Here's a nigger to help you. Now I want this done tonight. I am not to be hung or even tried. I want this done tonight without fail. Go out there at first dark. The other crowd will be here between eight and nine o'clock—he never called no names—but don't you boys wait on them. Go there at first dark and get them at the supper table. Jump right in and shoot them down and cut the little ones' throats.

"He said again he would give me a hundred dollars to kill Mr. Carter and Mrs. Carter, and a thirty-two caliber Smith and Wesson pistol to kill the two older children. Then he sits down there in the house and he said, 'Now, I want this done without fail,' as I took hold of the watermelon. He asked me, 'You ain't got no knife?' I said, 'No, sir.' He pulled out his knife and gave it to me. I took the knife and cut the watermelon. He said, 'I have got to go to town,' and when he said that, I handed his knife back to him.

"He said, 'No, keep the knife. I want you to kill every God-damned one of them and set the place afire. Use the knife to slit the throats of the little ones when they run out and throw them back in the fire. Then you get the mules and ride them three or four miles so the dogs can't follow you. Take the bridles off them and walk back to the shanty. I can't get into town in time to get the money today, but I will have it tomorrow. When you see a man on a gray horse, that will be me. If you see anybody else, you get up and go toward the house.'

"Then he said, 'Be careful to get no bloodstains on your clothes. If you do, I will get you some more clothes and you must burn the bloody clothes. When I get here, you take the hundred dollars and walk through the country to Alapaha. Then you get on the train and ride as far as the money will carry you. You are not to be seen again. I know they will arrest me. I will be suspicioned because I done shot him.'

"Then he said to the boys, 'Give this Negro Tim McDonald's gun. Mine is notched out because of the way I shoot, and if you was to get in a tight and drop my gun, it would betray me.' So they give me a single-barrel breech-loader.

"He said to me, 'Now after I go, you get out and walk around so you'll know where to go tonight.' So I walks from the shanty to the tram road and down to the Carter place. I set down my gun in a fence corner and walked on up to Mr. Carter's place. Mr. Carter was laying down on the front porch."

Moore told about an amicable exchange with Carter. He told Carter he was looking for the road to Cat Creek. After directions were given, Moore said he walked back to the corner of the fence, picked up the gun and started down the road.

"I saw Willie Carter plowing and I spoke to him. He asked me if I was hunting a job. I said no, and then I stood there and talked to Willie for some little time."

Moore said he scouted the Carter layout from both sides and arrived back at the shanty at about sundown. "I stays there until the moon commenced to get up...and the Rawlins boys walks in—Leonard, Milton and Jesse. They brought two guns with them. We sits there just a little while and then Milton said, 'It's time to go.' Then we goes to Mr. Carter's house.

"We headed up that way, me and Jesse walking side by side. We come to the house, within seven or eight feet of the corner of the house. Mrs. Carter was coming back from the kitchen. Jesse throwed the gun on Mrs. Carter, and I caught it and said, 'Don't. Don't do that. I can't.' I held the gun down and Mrs. Carter comes out (of the kitchen) and goes on in the house. We went around the house looking and then we came back to where Jesse started to shoot Mrs. Carter. Then Milton starts to go inside the kitchen and the dog hailed him. The dog barked and Milton started backing and he kept backing until he got around the smokehouse.

"Willie, Mr. Carter's son, gets up inside the house and comes to the back door (with a rifle in his hands). Jesse Rawlins peeped around the smokehouse and Willie shot. Willie hissed his dog but it kept barking and we kept backing away. Willie come around the smokehouse and shot his gun again. His father says, 'Willie, what are you doing? You're gonna kill that motherless calf.' Willie said, 'Pa, I see'd a man.' His father said, 'Willie, come back.' We were backed under a tree and when Willie stepped around a fig tree, a gun fired, bam! Willie fell back on the ground and said, 'Oh . . .'

"His little sister screamed and ran to him, and she said, 'Willie, what's going on? Are you hurt?' The gun fired again, a big fog of smoke, and she never said a word after that.

"I heard Mr. Carter say, 'Give me my gun, give me my gun. They're coming in the house!' Milton and Jesse, they jumps the fence and runs through the yard around to the other side of the house. Me and Leonard was standing in the horse lot and I see'd Willie get up. When Milton and Jesse goes around the house, he goes behind them. He went plumb around, going behind them, until he get to the front door. He called his mother to let him in, and I heard her say, 'Lord have mercy!'

"Then Mrs. Carter called the name of the girl who was killed, and then I heard Mr. Carter say, 'Don't go out there. They'll kill you.' I heard Willie ask for a doctor, and I heard this girl ask her father to let her go get some help. He told her not to go, that they would kill her, too.

"I heard Willie ask them to get a doctor. But Milton was standing at the door on this side and Jesse was standing at the door on the south side. They were standing with their guns presented, right at the house. Milton walks back to me, breaks the gun and drops the shell in the horse lot. He puts in another shell and says, 'Go in there and kill every God-damned one in there. There's a thousand, fifteen hundred dollars in there. Go through the house and get all of that, then come out and fire the house.'

"I got the gun in my hand and Milton is standing in front of me. I looked at it (the gun) and I looked at him and I said, 'I ain't a-goin' in that house.' He said, 'You ain't done a God-damned thing tonight, and if you don't finish the job, I'll see that the old man don't give you one cent of that hundred dollars he promised you.' I said, 'I'm leaving here. This is getting too God-damned hot. You're gonna fool around and that old man is going to kill some of you.'

"Jesse was standing there, and he said, 'I can get 'em out.' He sits his gun down and gets some shucks and carries them to the side of the door and lays them down. He comes back and gets another armload and starts back through the front gate. When he does that, Mr. Carter shot. Jesse drops the shucks and comes back to us boys. 'Did he hit you?' Milton asked, and he (Jesse) said 'No.'

"I said, 'Boys, I'm leaving here I can't do this.' Leonard tells me to shut my God-damned mouth. Then I said it again, 'I ain't doing this. I'm leaving here.' And that time I darts around the crib, and I left there. I went through Mr. Carter's cotton patch, and I come to a log back there. I sit down there on that log until way after midnight. When I went off, I carried my gun with me, the one I got from Mr. Rawlins. It was the gun Milton fired when the children was killed.

"I carried that gun to Staunton, to my shanty. I laid it on my bunk and covered it with quilts. When I was arrested, I told them where the gun was, and they went and got it."

The prosecutor finished questioning Moore a few minutes after seven o'clock, and Judge Mitchell adjourned court for the day.

Attorney Cooper showed up Wednesday morning ready to discredit Moore's testimony. But Moore was often evasive or vague with his answers. At times, he even seemed to be toying with the defense attorney.

"Have you ever served time in the penitentiary?" Cooper asked.

Moore: "I don't know. Do you know?"

Red-faced, the attorney asked the judge to direct the witness to answer the question. The judge told Moore to answer.

"No, sir, I don't know nothing about a penitentiary."

"But you served time in Tennessee?"

"Not that I know of."

Again, Cooper asked the judge to direct the witness to answer the question, saying that Moore surely knew whether he had served time in the Tennessee penitentiary. The judge told the witness that if he knew the answer, he was obliged to answer it truthfully and accurately.

Moore smiled and said, "No, sir, I never spent no time in the Tennessee penitentiary."

Cooper: "But you have been arrested?"

Moore: "Yes, sir. Now I have been arrested. I recall that."

Cooper: "How many times?"

Moore: "I really don't know."

Again the attorney asked the judge for a definitive answer. The judge told Moore to answer if he knew how many times he had been arrested.

Moore: "I couldn't tell you how many times I've been arrested. I was arrested here in Lowndes County by the marshal. And I was arrested in Brooks (County). But I don't know how many times. It was always for cursing, getting drunk, that sort of thing. I never served no time in the Georgia or Tennessee penitentiary."

Cooper (alluding to a rumor that Moore was once arrested for murder in Coffee County): "Ever been arrested for murder?"

Moore: "Not until this case here."

Cooper: "Never?"

Moore (smiling): "Colonel, I been arrested a good number of times, but never for murder, never for anything that would put me in the penitentiary."

Cooper: "But you have been arrested – what did you call it? – a good number of times?"

Moore (still smiling): "Yes, sir, I said that – a good number of times."

Cooper's next bit of strategy was to try to show that Moore's confession was made under duress, that he was told he might be lynched if he didn't tell the story at the time he was arrested. He asked Moore to tell about his arrest.

"I was at Staunton when the officers found me. I was walking to the commissary from the shanty. It was the Saturday after the killing. I walks up to the commissary and Mr. Ivey (Moore's employer) walks out on the front porch with them – Mr. Passmore and Mr. Crosby. Mr. Crosby had a shotgun, and the sheriff had a gun, too. The sheriff said, 'Hands up.' I never resisted or tried to run and dodge. I put my hands up.

"He puts the handcuffs on me, and I said, 'What you want with me?' He said, 'Be quiet and I'll tell you.' Then he said, 'But right now, we're just going to carry you to town.' I wasn't no fool. I knew what they wanted me for. They didn't have to tell me. Then he said, 'We're carrying you to town in a case of murder.' And Mr. Passmore didn't say anything else to me, and Mr. Crosby didn't say anything else to me, just that they was carrying me to town in the case of murder.

"I told Mr. Ivey that I would tell what I knew, and he said, 'Alf, there was a crowd in Hahira going to lynch you, and I turned around and come back."

Cooper: "That's what he said to you in the presence of the officers, that there was a crowd that was going to lynch you?'

Moore: "Mr. Passmore and Mr. Crosby, they never said nothing. I said nothing to them. Mr. Ivey is the one that said there was a crowd that wanted to lynch me."

Cooper: "But you were scared?"

Moore: "No, sir, they didn't scare me nary a bit. I haven't been scared at all in this case."

Cooper, obviously frustrated that he didn't get the admission he sought, said, "OK, go on with your testimony."

Moore: "Well, I stayed there until train time. Don't know how long it was, an hour or so, I guess. No one was talking seriously to me all that time. No one. I didn't tell the whole truth until I knew I was secure in jail."

Cooper: "How come you made a confession?"

Moore: "They come to me and asked me for the truth, and I told them. That was last week. Before that, I told them some other tale. What I told them wasn't the whole truth. I told all kinds of tales in jail here."

Cooper: "When was it that you made this confession to the officers implicating J.G. Rawlins and his sons? At Staunton?"

Moore: "Wasn't talking about Mr. Rawlins at Staunton. I just said I will tell you. But I didn't tell them. I didn't tell them anything until I seen I was secure in jail here in Valdosta and then I didn't tell the whole truth – what I told on the stand yesterday – until last week."

Cooper: "They came there with guns, and Mr. Ivey told you this crowd was about to lynch you, and you knew you didn't have any protection. And you didn't tell them anything?"

Moore: "They never scared me at all. I wasn't any more scared then than I am now, and I ain't scared now. The reason I made a confession, they come and asked me. Nobody deceived me, nobody scared me, nobody made no threats toward me."

Cooper: "Didn't you tell them on the train that Mr. Rawlins hired you to kill the Carters?"

Moore, "No, sir. We just sat on the train. I didn't say anything like what you just said."

Cooper: "Then you swear you never told them anything about this crime until you had been put in jail here in Valdosta."

Moore: "Yes, sir, that's what I'm swearing to."

Cooper: "Did anyone come to your cell last night and talk to you about the testimony you gave yesterday, that maybe you made a mistake here and there and you ought to try to get it right?"

Moore: "No, sir. Nobody went to my cell and talked to me since I went off the stand yesterday afternoon. I talked to the niggers in jail with me. I think there's nine of them. I told them what I told on the stand, but no one else talked to me. No, sir, I didn't talk to no one 'cept the niggers in jail with me. That's all."

Cooper then took Moore back over his arrest and tried once again to get him to admit he was scared of being lynched when he made the confession to his employer, but Moore was adamant that he held no fear of being lynched.

Finally, the attorney walked to the defense table, conferred with attorney Smith and Joe and Milton Rawlins. Then he turned to the judge and said, "No more questions, your honor."

The solicitor, not wanting the riveting testimony by Moore to be watered down by the lengthy cross-examination, covered all of the high points of the confession again and covered some new ground, too. He asked Moore how he first made contact with Rawlins to do the killing.

Moore: "First word told to me come from Berry Sirmans (Moore's co-worker at the cross-tie camp). He told me that Mr. Rawlins wakes him up in the night and told him he would give a hundred dollars to kill Mr. Carter. Berry said, 'I told Mr. Rawlins I wouldn't do it.'

"Well, it rocked on for about two weeks. Then Mitch Johnson from down in Hahira came to me. I was sitting in front of the commissary when he burst out in a big laugh and said, 'Alf, I got a message to deliver to you. Frank Turner wants to see you down in Hahira.' So I rode the Shoo-Fly down to Hahira and talked to Frank. Frank tells me that Mr. Rawlins told him that if he would bring him a man that would kill Mr. Carter, Frank would get twenty-five dollars and a new suit of clothes. I ran into Mr. Rawlins Saturday night and he told me to come out to his place Tuesday morning to talk."

Finally satisfied, Thomas turned his star witness back to the defense.

On recross-examination, Cooper bore down on inconsistencies in Moore's testimony, grilling him again about how much he confessed the day he was arrested. He said he thought about telling his part in the crime to store owner Briggs Lawson in Hahira the morning after the killings. "But I was afraid they might put me on a limb, if I started talking about it right then. So I came back to Staunton. And when Mr. Ivey asked me about it, I told him that I was there (at the Carter house). He called the sheriff."

In his testimony, Moore cited date after date on which details of the tragedy unfolded, and then Cooper asked, "Ain't it true that you have a hard time remembering dates? You can't remember when I'm questioning you, but they become crystal clear when the solicitor is asking the questions."

Moore smiled and said, "I carried them dates. Mother wit schooled me. I have no education. I cannot read or write. But I can remember dates when something important happened."

Then Cooper asked the question that was on everybody's mind: "Tell us, Alf. What kind of deal did you work out to give this testimony? Are you going to just get up and walk out of here when the trials are over?"

Moore: "Nobody give me to understand that I wouldn't be prosecuted. They didn't give me any hopes. Nobody has told me that they would help me out of this case or that I would be protected from prosecution. They have treated me as well as jail prisoners can expect to be treated, but I ain't had no promises."

During Cooper's questioning, Moore's testimony refuted court officials' belief that Joe Bentley was involved in the murders. At one point, Moore said, "Joe Bentley was not with me (when he went to the Carter house in the afternoon). He never was with me. He's in jail here charged in this crime, but he never was with me. If he got involved in it, I don't know how."

That testimony eventually freed Bentley. Passmore later said the case against Bentley "was pretty thin," and if any effort were made to continue to prosecute him, then all of Moore's testimony might have been discounted. So it was easier to free Bentley than having to deal with that possibility.

Moore's testimony may also have prevented Jim McDonald from being charged. "I didn't see anybody else there besides the Rawlins boys. I didn't see Tim McDonald or Jim McDonald there. There was just me and the three boys."

During Cooper's questioning, Moore made a chilling statement that removed any doubt about his part in the crime. "I accepted the terms of a hundred dollars to kill out a whole family. I was going to kill them for money just like Mr. Rawlins ordered. He never forced me to do it. He wasn't standing there over me with a gun. I went there of my own free will and accord."

Moore was excused from the stand after more than five hours of testimony and cross-examinations.

11

ELLA CARTER, MOTHER OF THE MURDERED CHILDREN, WAS next called to the witness stand. Dressed in black and wearing a black hat without a veil, she carried herself erect. The only sound was the whisper of her long dress brushing the courtroom floor as she walked to the witness stand. She answered questions in a soft but confident voice.

She corroborated the accounts previously given by her husband and Alf Moore. She said she could not see who the shooters were, but she positively identified Jesse Rawlins as one of two men running across the yard shortly after the shooting. She said the duo passed within four or five paces of her, but she recognized only Jesse.

She recounted her son's dying statement that Jesse and Milton Rawlins fired the shots that hit him and Carrie. With some emotion in her voice but without breaking into sobs, she described her son's wounds.

"I put my hand there," she said as utter silence blanketed the audience, "and felt the blood oozing out of his side, just above his pants. The shots didn't remain in him. They went through and came out the back just above his belt. He lived until sunup the next morning."

A gasp was heard when she described the condition of her daughter's body the next morning as "all shot to pieces... stamped on the face...her ear either snatched off or shot off... the print of shoe tacks on her wrist."

In cross-examination, attorney Cooper, who had unmercifully attacked the testimony of previous witnesses, was less aggressive with Ella Carter, but he was persistent nonetheless.

In perhaps her most important testimony, Mrs. Carter said firmly, "Willie Carter's dying statement was that Milton and Jesse done the shooting that killed him and Carrie, that Jesse shot him and Milton shot my little girl."

Even without being overly aggressive, Cooper drew one statement from Mrs. Carter that seemed to help the defense. When Cooper pressed the witness about identifying Alf Moore as being the black man at the scene, she replied, "I would not begin to say whether I could identify him under such circumstances. It was a dark night. It was a moon-shiny night, but it was dark. It would have been pretty hard for me to have identified anybody out there that night."

When Cooper asked if it was difficult to identify Moore, why was she so certain about the others, she said, "Two of them ran right by me, and I saw Leonard later standing in the clear moonlight."

"With Alf Moore? Right?"

"Well, it turns out that it was him, I guess. He confessed to being there. Isn't that what I read in the paper? But I didn't identify him as being there. I couldn't make that statement truthfully."

Ella Carter also described the ill feeling that permeated that part of Lowndes County. "I never did have any trouble with the McDonalds. My child, Willie, has. The Rawlins boys and Jim McDonald met him off at the river and give him a beating. That was a year before the killing. They (the McDonalds) were our enemies...(they) didn't speak...(but) lived within three hundred yards of us. They plowed within fifty feet of my gate. We were living there, deadly enemies to each other...all of us—my husband and myself and McDonald and his wife—enemies, that is true."

On two occasions in her testimony, Mrs. Carter said her husband shot at Milton Rawlins. Carter had testified that he shot at Jesse. Cooper never challenged her on that point.

She was on the stand only about half an hour.

At half past eleven, Lora Carter, nineteen years old and the eldest of the Carter children, was called to the stand. She testified she was standing on the back steps of the house when the shots were fired. She was still standing on the back porch when two men, who came from where the shots were fired, jumped the fence and passed within ten paces of her. She identified them as Milton and Jesse Rawlins.

She also said she saw Leonard Rawlins and a black man she didn't know, and one time, when she was peeking through a crack, Milton Rawlins was peeking back at her from the other side of the same crack. She also swore that she saw both Tim and Jim McDonald at some point during the siege.

Attorney Cooper fired a barrage of questions at her, but he apparently didn't shake her testimony. She calmly and politely replied to each of his questions. When Cooper became exasperated with her answers, his voice rose and became harsh at one point. Then he caught himself and apologized for "hollering" at her. Miss Carter accepted the apology, but said, "Don't do it again."

Most everyone in the courtroom, including Cooper, smiled at her admonition. Cooper then said, "No more questions," and Judge Mitchell called a recess.

First witness in the afternoon session was Ella Jones, who was living on the nearby John Dasher farm at the time of the killings. She said she lived about a mile from the Carter place and perhaps half a mile from the Rawlins house.

"I was home that night (June 13th). The first thing that attracted my attention was hollering and screaming...from both houses, first from Mr. Carter's house and then from the Rawlins house. I heard it from both places. It was ladies doing the screaming. But we didn't go to either place. I didn't want my husband to go, and I wasn't going to go, either. There had been just too much trouble to go out at night.

"I know about the J.G Rawlins place. I worked there. I did hoeing, picking cotton and the like. And I heard Milton make statements relative to the Carters. A year ago this spring...I was putting out compost when he told Jodie, my husband, that if he would promise to go with him, he would get up a crowd and furnish the guns. He said that, before he would allow Carter to stay there, they would kill the whole family from the baby up. He said he would shoot off the door locks if Jodie would help him take the whole Carter family out. That's exactly what he said—take them all out. He said it in the field and he said it at the house one day."

Cross-examination of Mrs. Jones brought a bit of levity to the trial. The *Macon Telegraph* carried this account:

"Mrs. Jones was put under a rigid cross-examination and became very impatient with attorney Cooper. When asked if the distance between her house and the Rawlinses was not more than a mile, she replied, 'I've told you once that it was about a mile, and if you don't believe what I said, go measure it for yourself.'

"Questioned about the time she went to bed that night, she replied, 'When I got ready...and I got up in the morning at the same time.' Asked to be specific about the time she got up in the morning, she replied, 'When I took a notion'."

Cooper painted Mrs. Jones as a gossip and asked her if she hadn't talked to so many people and repeated the story so many times that she had "made a song out of it." Indignantly, Mrs. Jones denied it. Asked if she was mad because she was ordered off the Rawlins property and her house given to another farm worker, she hotly denied that allegation, too.

The prosecution then sent a parade of witnesses to the stand that was meant to tie the shotgun and knife found in Alf Moore's shanty to Joe Rawlins.

W.E. Martin, Rawlins' closest neighbor, identified a Barlow knife found in Moore's possession as the same one he saw

Jodie Jones swap to Rawlins for a bone-handled knife on Sunday before the murders.

Under cross-examination by Cooper, Martin said it "certainly resembled" the knife in the swap, but he conceded there were many of the two-bladed Barlows that looked identical. He said he couldn't be "one hundred percent positive" that it was the same knife. The tip of one of the blades was broken off when he saw it in the sheriff's possession. "It wasn't broken at the time of the swap," he said. "Mr. Rawlins gave him twenty cents to boot on the swap. I don't believe he would have done that if the blade had been broken."

Ed Duggan, another farmer, said he also had seen the knife and believed that it was the same one Jodie Jones had owned in the spring. Under cross-examination, he, too, said he could not be absolutely certain it was the same knife.

E.L. Ivey, who lived in Valdosta but operated his cross-tie business in Staunton, took the stand next. He was Alf Moore's employer at the time of the crime.

"Alf Moore was not at my camp on June 13th. He left there on Saturday and was not back on Monday. He came back on Wednesday or Thursday. I found that knife in his shanty on a shelf—where he told me to go and get it. I know about that gun (which Moore had previously identified). I found it in his bunk between the slats and mattress. I found a shell with the gun. It was loaded. I delivered the knife and gun to the officers, Mr. Crosby and Mr. Passmore, when Alf was arrested."

Under cross-examination, Ivey said, "I don't know where that Negro came from. I don't know if I ever asked him. He worked for me about four years and then he left for a while. He came back to work for me in March, I believe. He worked for me up to the time he was arrested.

"How'd we come to find the gun? Alf told me where to go and get it. He told me when he was arrested at the commissary. He told me partly about the crime and he told me right off that he had a gun. And he told me where to go and get it. The sheriff knew he had a gun. He asked about it, and the Negro said it was in his shanty.

"I told Alf, 'I planned your capture. I didn't want any of my hands in the camp getting hurt. I did it this way hoping that no one would get hurt. I figured if you were guilty, you would tell the truth about what happened.' Then he began telling his story to Mr. Passmore, his deputy and me. He told part of the story and said he would tell the rest later on. He implicated the Rawlinses the first time he told the story.

"Who was there? The sheriff was standing there with his shotgun. The deputy had a gun, too, and he was standing over him (Moore) while he was telling the story."

Solicitor Thomas obviously wasn't happy about the last scene described by the witness. It suggested the confession might have been given under duress. Thomas asked that the testimony be stricken from the record, but the judge overruled the motion. Even so, Cooper knew it would be a strong point in an appeal if his clients were convicted. Both Cooper and Joe Rawlins were hastily scribbling notes as Ivey testified.

Questioned about how he knew Alf Moore had a gun in his shanty, Ivey said, "Alf was the first to tell me that he had Rawlins' gun. I asked him about it after some of the Negroes there in the quarters said he had been walking about with a gun on his shoulder. I think it was Mitch Johnson that told me Alf had a gun."

Fifteen-year-old Jim McDonald took the stand next and immediately identified the shotgun found in Moore's shanty as one that Joe Rawlins had picked up at the McDonald house about twelve hours before the Carter children were killed. "I guess it belonged to Mr. Rawlins," he said. "It had been around our house for a long time, but Mr. Rawlins said it belonged to him. He left one with us that has a notched-out stock. It's notched out because he has just one eye and he has to lay his head across the stock when he shoots."

Under cross-examination, he said his father, a brother-in-law of Sheriff Passmore, and Carter "were deadly enemies and still are. They have not made up since this killing." He also testified that he heard three gunshots that evening as he sat on his porch shortly after dark but he did not investigate. "I didn't hear any more shooting and I didn't hear any hollering. I went to bed pretty early," he said.

Young McDonald also offered a flat denial about being seen at the Carter house with a gun.

The state's tenth witness was Deputy Sheriff Crosby, who described physical evidence he and an investigator, D. F. Fleming, gathered. He said he didn't look for tracks between the two houses on Wednesday, but he went back the following day. He said he found four sets of tracks leading across the field toward the Carter house and only three sets going the other way. One of the sets of tracks was peculiar he said. One brogan was missing a heel and left distinctive nail marks. However, no effort was made to match those to the marks on the dead girl's arm, he said.

Under cross-examination, he said he did not measure the footprints, but said they "looked like the tracks of the boys who had been thinning corn in Mr. Rawlins' field."

Crosby also testified that, after Alf Moore told his story, he went to the shanty on Joe Rawlins' farm and found the watermelon rinds Moore had mentioned. He also searched the Rawlins home and found a zinc bucket with a dent near the bottom of it, exactly as Alf Moore had described it to investigators.

Under cross-examination, he said he did not have a search warrant to enter the Rawlins home. "I don't know whether it was the solicitor or the sheriff that instructed me to search Rawlins' house, but one of them did. Otherwise, I wouldn't have done it."

J. J. Boone, a Carter neighbor, was the eleventh state witness. He testified about following the tracks through the fields the morning after the killings. He said he found four sets coming to the Carter house and three sets going the other way.

Sheriff Passmore was next, and he, too, described the tracks he saw leading to the Carter house. He also said that, after hearing Alf's story about running away from the house, he found a set of tracks leading across a cotton field and into a stand of pine trees. "They were made by someone who was running," he said.

The sheriff spent less than ten minutes testifying for the state, but Cooper's cross-examination lasted almost an hour. First, Cooper got an admission from the sheriff that he did not follow the tracks toward the Rawlins house. "I didn't have time," he said. "I had prisoners under arrest and wanted to make it to the train station before it came down."

Cooper also established that a sprinkling of rain had fallen on Wednesday night, and perhaps the tracks had been obliterated somewhat before Crosby went back and followed them.

Asked why he went to Staunton to look for Moore, the sheriff said, "Mr. Carter told us there was a strange Negro in this trouble. Mr. Ivey came down to Valdosta to talk to me about where the strange Negro was. He said some of the Negroes in the camp told him that Alf Moore had been back there since Wednesday, walking around with a gun on his shoulder.

"No, sir, Mr. Carter never said there were two Negroes in it. We've got three Negroes in jail right now. One of them is Frank Turner, who was indicted. I do not know whether Joe Bentley is implicated in this or not. But we're still holding him in jail."

Cooper went into great detail about the arrests and asked the sheriff if it was true that he held the defendants for more than a month without arrest warrants. The sheriff said no warrants were taken for any of the defendants until the grand jury met. "I arrested them on my own hook," the sheriff said testily. "I have arrested men—I've arrested two white men—before for murder and never had no arrest warrant."

Passmore confirmed that he put the two younger Rawlins boys in a cell away from their father and older brother, but he denied that he tried to get a confession from either. With that on the record, Passmore was asked to denounce a newspaper report to the contrary.

Passmore: "I did not take Jesse out of his prison cell and try to get him to confess. There's not a word of truth to it."

Cooper: "That is a mistake by the newspaper then? You never did try to get a confession out of Leonard either?"

Passmore: "I never asked any such question of Leonard. I never asked Jesse a thing. It is true that he (Crosby) went in there to talk to them several times. I could not tell you whether he took them out of the cell. I don't think he did. Now I've been in Alf Moore's cell. I talked to him three or four times."

A quick succession of witnesses followed the sheriff, none of them testifying for more than a few minutes. Their testimony supported earlier statements by state witnesses about movements and associations of the men charged in the crime.

J. Y. Blitch, a bank teller, testified Joe Rawlins borrowed $110 from the bank on the morning of June 14, corroborating Moore's statement that he would have to go to the bank to get the money to pay him.

Robert Dye, a livery stable employee, testified he drove Rawlins to the Double Bridges area, within walking distance of Rawlins' house on Wednesday morning after the murders.

J.A. Stubbs, a Carter neighbor, testified to seeing Moore in the vicinity of the Carter house the afternoon before the murders. He also said he talked to the Rawlins boys who were plowing. He said, "They were not nervous a bit, neither of them. They never made me believe they were going to do anything from the way they appeared."

G.B. Jones of Hahira swore he saw Alf Moore and Frank Turner in deep conversation in Hahira on Saturday before the killings.

C.W. Webb, a Hahira merchant, testified Rawlins left a watermelon at his store on the afternoon before the killings and said Frank Turner would pick it up later. Turner came and got it about eight o'clock.

"He'd taken the watermelon out of the store," Webb said. "I don't know whether he ate it. I did not get any of it."

Laughter rippled through the courtroom as Solicitor Thomas said, "Your honor, the state rests."

Milton Rawlins smiled.

Attorney Cooper, his white shirt soaked with perspiration, propped his head in his hands as if in prayer.

Joe Rawlins leaned back in his chair and looked upward.

It was half past six o'clock, and Judge Mitchell called a halt to proceedings until Thursday morning.

12

JOHN RANDOLPH COOPER BEGAN HIS DEFENSE OF MILTON Rawlins by telling the jury he would prove the Rawlins boys were home with their mother and sisters on the night of the murders.

"So many lies have been told and so many misstatements have been made," he said, "that it will take time, gentlemen of the jury, to ferret out the truth. But please bear with me and consider every detail in the testimony presented in the defense of Milton Rawlins. He has been falsely accused, and it should be obvious by now that this fine young man is either a most cold-blooded kind of killer or he is being railroaded. He's being railroaded. Why? Someone must hang for these tragic murders, and he just happens to be very convenient because of a long-running feud between his family and the Carters. So please listen to these witnesses and consider their testimony as it is presented."

That said, he began calling witnesses to impeach both the testimony and character of W.L. Carter.

First witness for the defense, W.W. Webb, postmaster at Hahira, testified about an incident involving Carter's mailbox. He said Carter demanded a report be made to postal officials that Tim McDonald's son and Ben Rice's son had tampered with his mailbox. After an inspector came down from Macon and inspected the mailbox, Carter tried to withdraw the report. Webb said it had gone too far, and he wouldn't withdraw it. Carter became angry and cursed him, Webb said.

Webb also testified he believed "the general character of Mr. Carter is bad."

However, he stopped short of saying that he absolutely would not believe Carter under oath.

Ben C. Rice, a farmer who lived a couple of miles from Carter, testified he would not believe Carter under oath. But he also admitted under cross-examination that he and the Rawlinses were "good friends."

Lee Fiveash, another Rawlins acquaintance, said he saw the Rawlins boys plowing about half an hour before sundown. "Leonard was at the house and we ate some watermelon. Jesse and Milton came in. I do not know how long I stayed there, but it was getting dark when I left." That testimony was meant to rebut Moore's testimony concerning the time he said the boys arrived at the shanty.

L. L. Webb, Hahira businessman, was the fourth defense witness. He testified that Carter was trying to buy cotton and Webb offered Carter the use of his scales and warehouse. "He seemed to have considerable money there at Hahira on that particular day. He told me he had a right smart amount, plenty to do his business. He showed his money around there to let people know he had money to buy cotton when they brought it in.

"Is his character good or bad? I always considered it not the best. If there was not some other fact connected with his oath to make me believe it, I would not."

Next witness was Dan Passmore, brother of the sheriff and the caller who first alerted lawmen about the murder. "I was at the Carter home the day after the killing. I was on the coroner's jury and I heard testimony in the case. I inquired as to who was there. Mr. Carter said Leonard was not there. I inquired of his daughter and Mrs. Carter the same thing, and they said Leonard was not there. They all said Milton and Jesse and two Negroes were there. Later, I heard talk about someone maybe having a smutty face, but the Carters didn't tell me that.

"I know the general character of Mr. Carter. His character is bad. I would not believe him under oath."

Under cross-examination by the prosecutor, Passmore described his relationship with the Rawlinses as "very friendly," and added, "They are good people, very accommodating, good neighbors."

Arlin Register, a farmer who lived near the feuding families, also was on the coroner's jury and he testified that Carter did not mention Leonard as one of the attackers, mentioning only "Milton and Jesse and two Negroes."

T. J. Simmons, a reporter for the *Valdosta Times* who had earlier written a story quoting the Carters as saying one of the attackers might have been a white man with a smutty face, said he stood by his story as being accurate.

In an attempt to discredit testimony by the Carters, Cooper recalled W.L. Carter and Lora Carter back to the witness stand and asked them if they had made a statement to the reporter about one of their attackers having a "smutty face." Both denied they had said it.

"I will explain it this way," the father of the dead children said. "He (Simmons) asked me, was one of their faces smutty that night? I said, 'No, sir.' He said, 'Ain't there been such a report?' I told him there had been all sorts of rumors and reports."

Lora Carter said flatly, "I never told him anything at all about one of the boys' faces being smutty."

Simmons was called back to the stand and testified, "My recollection is that statement was made by somebody there, that they did not know whether it was a white man with a smutty face or a Negro."

Lola Rawlins, thirteen-year-old sister of the defendant, was called to the stand. She testified that Milton and Jesse were plowing in the field all day and she had been "dropping peas" for them to cover. "They came to the house at about sundown," she said. "I saw Milton and Jesse go to their room and go to bed. They were there all night. Leonard stayed up for a while."

On cross-examination, she was asked if her mother had been upset on the night of the killings and had been crying.

Miss Rawlins: "My mother was not crying that night that I know about. She didn't have anything to cry about. I know that my mother was awake a good part of the night, but I don't know that she was crying."

Thomas: "Didn't your mother and sister, time and time again during the night, go to the door and look out. Didn't she wait for the boys to come back until nearly daybreak?"

Miss Rawlins: "No, sir, they was never gone for them to have to come back."

Leila Rawlins, fifteen-year-old sister of the defendant, was called to the stand. She corroborated her sister's testimony, saying Milton and Jesse went to bed about nine o'clock that night and did not leave the house. She said she was awake until half past eleven o'clock and she did not hear any shooting the night of the murders.

Angeline Rawlins was called to the witness stand. Dozens of women were in the courtroom audience and hundreds more were among the throngs outside the courthouse. It was obvious, a *Valdosta Times* report said, that more women related to Mrs. Rawlins than related to Mrs. Carter. Although a little plump after bearing five children, the mother of the defendant carried herself well at age forty and other women flocked to her side as she passed through the crowd to get into the courthouse. Some spoke words of encouragement; some just wanted to pat her shoulder. Mrs. Rawlins tried to acknowledge the comments and show of affection, but it was sometimes overwhelming.

"What is it about her that makes her stand out?" one woman asked aloud.

"She's got class," said another.

People in the courtroom fell into complete silence as Mrs. Rawlins began to speak.

"I am the mother of Milton Rawlins, now on trial for his life. My husband is sitting over there. That one-armed man is my father, J. J. Jowers. I come from Coffee County. I moved to Lowndes County a little more than eight years ago."

Then she, too, said that her sons had plowed all day and were at home all evening. Her husband, she added, had gone to Valdosta on business and spent the night there. "I can account for my sons' whereabouts from the time they got home from plowing in the fields until the next morning. They were in the house, my house."

She also denied reports that she ever said the boys had gone 'coon hunting that night. "I never said any such thing," she testified. "We never let them go 'coon hunting."

On cross-examination, she said she checked on the boys late in the night and could see Milton asleep in his bed. She estimated the time at one o'clock.

E.C. Bruffey, a reporter for the *Atlanta Constitution*, was next called by the defense as an expert witness. He said he had been "put to the test of trying to identify a person by moonlight" and he had found it very difficult if not impossible to identify people in the shadows of trees.

Cooper: "Is it possible or not to recognize a Negro or a white man twenty to thirty yards away?"

Bruffey: "Well, if it was open in the moonlight, one probably could. But the test I was put to was identifying parties passing under trees. One would have to have mighty good vision to identify a person moving under moonlight if those persons were twenty yards away and passing under a tree. It is a hard proposition to distinguish the color of a person at all."

After Cooper laid out a scenario, Bruffey said, "I have very good eyesight, (but) I don't know if it is possible for a person to identify a person as Negro or white, twenty or thirty yards away, looking through a crack in the house, and only moonlight to see by. I would hate very much to attempt to do it and satisfy myself that I was correct in my conclusion."

Under cross-examination, Bruffey said it would be easier to recognize someone you knew than it would be to recognize a stranger.

The solicitor then asked, "That is your opinion as an expert?"

Bruffey: "I don't consider myself an expert. I just took the test to see if it was possible."

Next witness for the defense was H.E. Vansickle, a teacher from Valdosta who once taught near Hahira. "I am acquainted with the character of W.L. Carter, and (his) character is bad."

Under cross-examination, Vansickle said, "You might say I am related to Tim McDonald by marriage. He is my wife's uncle."

Milton Rawlins then took the stand to make a statement in his own defense.

"Gentlemen, I am not guilty of the charge...I am innocent of this if anybody was ever innocent of anything in this world. I was at home that night and I stayed there all night. We plowed until sundown and I knew nothing about this killing until after it happened.

"So far as Pa instructing me to bother Carter or his children or his stock or anything else, he has never done that. He always instructed me to leave him alone. I stayed at home sometimes to keep away from him.

"So far as the Negro is concerned, he is trying to swear my life away by swearing to lies. He swore to you that he told lies to the officers when they arrested him. He told some more here in this court."

The defendant finished his unsworn statement and left the stand. Since the statement was not made under oath, he could not be cross-examined.

Solicitor Thomas asked to reopen the case to hear two witnesses who had been overlooked earlier.

James Everett and Bill Plair, two men employed as guards soon after the arrests, testified they heard Mrs. Rawlins say outside the jail that her sons had gone 'coon hunting on the night of the killings.

Cooper brought Mrs. Rawlins back to the stand, and she again denied ever making the statement.

Both sides rested their cases.

Final arguments began. The prosecution and the defense were allowed two speakers each. For the prosecution, it would be Thomas and Whitaker; for the defense, Cooper and Smith.

Whitaker, assistant solicitor and the first to address the jury, took the testimony of Alf Moore and meshed it with corroborative evidence at numerous points. He declared that no human being could have manufactured such a web of evidence.

Then he detailed every movement of the principals in the case. He showed how the knife, the gun, the bucket and the watermelon rinds interlocked with different parts of Moore's testimony. Finally, he drew a graphic word-picture of the terror at the Carter home that night and urged the jury to return a verdict of guilty.

Smith followed for the defense and spoke for three hours. He launched a scathing attack on Alf Moore's testimony and painted him as the real murderer. "He lied when he was arrested. He lied when he arrived at the jail. He lied all the time he was in the jail. He lied on the witness stand. And he would lie again if he were brought into this court and asked what day of the week it is. He'd say anything but Friday. He has lied and robbed and murdered, and now he's trying to put an innocent man on the gallows.

"A dog should not have to hang on testimony offered up by a murderer like Alf Moore."

Smith didn't leave anybody out of his barrage of criticism—except maybe the judge.

He said prosecutors never uttered a word of condemnation for Moore, even though he lied to them, and the solicitor was "forced to withdraw evidence" that was based on Moore's testimony.

Solicitor Thomas rose and, his face flushed, said the evidence he withdrew was done on his own motion and added, "I didn't *have* to do it."

Smith harshly criticized the Carters and other state's witnesses, saying their testimony was prejudiced from the start. "This crime is so horrible," he said, "that there was a pressing need for a speedy conviction. My client just happened to be handy because he had disagreements with the Carters in the past."

Then he added, "The evidence points just as strongly to Tim and Jim McDonald as it does to Milton Rawlins." His voice rising, he asked, "Why did not the sheriff arrest them?"

Sheriff Passmore, a brother-in-law to Tim McDonald and Jim's uncle, jumped to his feet and replied with anger in his voice, "Because Old Man Carter did not say they were the guilty parties!" He shook his finger at Smith and added, "And the coroner's jury did not lay the crime to them, either!"

For a tense moment, the two men glared at one another across the courtroom, and even the judge seemed to be surprised at the sudden outburst by the sheriff. As the sheriff sank slowly back into his seat, his face still masked in anger, Smith said somewhat meekly that he wasn't accusing Tim McDonald of murder. "I was simply illustrating how unreliable circumstantial evidence can be," he added.

Mending fences even further, he said, "I want it understood that I am a friend of the sheriff and he is a friend of mine. I will not impugn his motives, but I must speak my convictions. There are not enough men living to muzzle me or drive me from the path of duty as I see it. Prejudice nailed the Lord to the cross, and others have suffered for it. You may hang me, ostracize me, lynch me, if you please, but you cannot keep me from going where I think my duty leads."

Taking a breather from that rapid-fire speech, Smith then retrieved his notes from the defense table and cited a long list of crimes where innocent men had been hanged. He added, "In a case like this where there was insufficient time to develop all of the facts," another innocent man might go to the gallows if the jury did not acquit Milton Rawlins.

Finally, he returned to the subject of Alf Moore, whom he described as "the black murderer who talked about the 'deppo,' the 'deppo,'" he said, mimicking Moore's way of pronouncing depot. "Confound a lying, fool Negro who comes around with such talk!"

From the defense table, Cooper gestured toward Smith and said, "He's trying to be polite."

"Politeness is not becoming of such a murderous villain," Smith said.

By the time Smith finished, the time was half past six o'clock. Judge Mitchell had indicated that he might hold a night session, but, at the request of Thomas and Cooper, he decided against it.

The heat in the courtroom had become unbearable, and spectators and officials alike were glad to vacate the ornate room.

Since the record throng on the streets had come prepared for a night session, most of them did not leave when the court day ended. The sheriff told a reporter for the *Macon Telegraph* that as many as two thousand people were on the streets of Valdosta at midnight. "I've never seen anything like it," he said.

Restaurants—several of which chose to join McCranie's Café as all-night establishments, at least until the trials ended—were packed to capacity as late as midnight.

Considering the reason for people gathering in Valdosta, the *Times* found it "ironic that the mood is festive, rather than somber."

At the home of O.M. Smith, attorney Cooper prepared for perhaps the most important closing argument of his career.

He told Smith that, if there was a stumbling block in this case, it was Alf Moore. Without Moore's testimony, Cooper believed they could discount everything else. Without his testimony to lend credence to Carter's and without Moore's testimony to tie the physical evidence together, the prosecution had very little on which to base a conviction.

He finally told Smith, "We have done all we can do. I'll just have to try to go after Moore's testimony tomorrow, tear it to smithereens. That's the best we can do."

A few blocks away, solicitor Thomas sat under an electric fan in his study and scribbled notes until early morning.

He felt good about the case, but he knew Cooper would offer a strong argument the next day. He genuinely admired the tall, athletic, forty-year-old attorney from Macon, and early the next morning, he confided to Whitaker that he wished Cooper were an ally instead of their adversary.

"He's going to give us a hell of a fight," Whitaker conceded. "And if we win this one, we'll have to do it three more times."

13

July 21, 1905

MORE THAN FOUR THOUSAND PEOPLE JAMMED THE DOWN-
town streets on Friday. A verdict was expected before the day
was out, and the crowd flowed about the courthouse like
waves of lava from an active volcano. They came as early as
seven o'clock to gawk at the main players in this drama being
acted out in their town.

Hundreds gathered on the east side of the courthouse to
see Milton and Joe Rawlins as they were escorted to court by
half a dozen deputies and jailers. The grim faces of the
lawmen contrasted sharply with the festive mood of the
crowd.

"Who's watching the jail?," a male voice called to the
lawmen.

A woman's voice from deep within the sea of humanity
said, "Maybe now is the time to break my worthless husband
out of jail." Hearty laughter greeted that remark.

"Hey, Milton, you don't look very worried," said another
male voice. "You reckon you're gonna be cleared?" Milton
Rawlins, showing little tension in spite of the situation,
smiled and nodded.

One man reached out as if to shake hands with Joe
Rawlins, but a deputy brushed the hand aside. Rawlins, his
hands handcuffed behind him, was hardly in a position to
accept the greeting, but he acknowledged the man by saying,
"Howdy, Otis."

Every seat in the courtroom was filled an hour before the 8:00 AM session was scheduled to begin. Electric fans stirred the air in the courtroom and the heat was tolerable.

The creaking of a door hinge brought a hush to the crowd just before the bailiff said, "All rise." Judge Mitchell entered and took his place on the bench. He regarded the crowd for a moment, then reminded those in the courtroom of rules he had established earlier in the trial. "Many of you are anticipating momentous events today," he said in a stern voice, "and I warn you again against any outbursts. The court will not tolerate any misconduct or demonstrations of any kind in this courtroom."

He then nodded at Cooper and told him to continue the closing arguments.

Cooper lifted his lanky frame from a chair at the defense table, turned to the jury and smiled, "Good morning, gentlemen." Most nodded and a few said quietly, "Good morning."

"First, gentlemen of the jury, let me say unequivocally that the state has made a wonderful case for the defendant." He paused for effect and then added, "You'll notice I said the state has made a wonderful case FOR Milton Rawlins. Other than the testimony of two unreliable witnesses, there is so little proof that he is involved in this atrocious crime that I am sure you will agree he is innocent."

Cooper then quoted a number of extracts from cases bearing similarities in which the defendant had been declared not guilty. And he noted that the case before the jury was unique.

"I can offer many references, but there never has been a case exactly like this one during my experience in the field of law. Nor could I find a case anywhere in America where a father was charged with sending his own flesh and blood—mere boys, at that—to commit murder. And, gentlemen, it didn't happen in this case, either. Milton

Rawlins is *not* guilty." His fist slammed the top of the defense table to punctuate the last sentence.

"I have practiced law in forty-two counties in the great state of Georgia, but this is by far the most unusual case I have ever taken. It has attracted more attention than any case in which I have been involved."

Cooper gazed around the courtroom, smiled and began heaping praise on various court officials. He complimented the judge on the conduct of the trial and praised the arguments before the jury on Thursday by his associate, O. M. Smith, as well as the assistant solicitor, G. A. Whitaker. "The only problem with Colonel Whitaker's presentation is that he is on the wrong side in this trial."

He also complimented the press on "fair treatment for all parties" during this trial. Then he turned to the jury and said, "Gentlemen, everyone involved in this trial has done their duty, done some good work. But if you hang Milton Rawlins, you will be doing the worst day's work of your lives and you will have disgraced yourselves and your county by putting an innocent young man on the gallows. I say again, Milton Rawlins is *not* guilty!"

And his fist slammed the top of the defense table to emphasize the last sentence.

Then he stopped as if to listen to some distant sound. He cupped a hand to his ear, and said to the judge, "Your honor, I would like for the electric fans to be turned off. A man's life hangs in the balance here today, and I don't want anything to interfere with what I have to say. I want every member of the jury to hear every word of every sentence, and I think the noise made by the fans might keep someone from hearing."

He paused and the judge nodded to a bailiff, who turned off the fans.

Cooper politely thanked the judge and the bailiff, but then the smile left his face as he launched an emotional campaign to save Milton Rawlins' life. He turned to the jury with a hurt expression on his face.

"Gentlemen, I have never seen—and we may never see again—such warm feelings by state's attorneys toward a self-convicted murderer and an admitted liar as we have seen here this week. I have never seen a nigger so important and held in such high esteem by white folks as we have seen here this week. It has been, 'Now Alf, tell us this' and 'Now Alf, tell us that.' Oh, such terms of warmth and feeling I have never heard before!

"I wouldn't want to have anything to do with a liar like this. He is the worst criminal that ever put a foot on Georgia soil. He would kill you as quick as he would kill a bird. He would kill a whole family and then go tell a pack of lies to hang someone else. Thank God he was not born in Georgia. You ought to hang him high and then send his body back to the state of Tennessee where he was born. He is too mean and too loathsome to rest upon Georgia soil. His dust would pollute the good soil of our grand old state."

Cooper paused and wiped his brow with a handkerchief as he warmed to the task. The temperature in the courtroom also was rising. Still, he did not ask that the fans be turned back on. As the lawyer's perspiration sometimes dripped onto the defense table, Milton would smile, seemingly pleased and entertained by his attorney's passionate performance.

"This Negro, this lying, murdering Negro, has told a story on these white folks that has startled the whole state of Georgia," Cooper said. "Everybody is talking about it because he brought innocent white folks into it. He says he never told the truth until he was put on the stand. But he was trained. The state took time to prime their witness just like you'd prime a pump. No nigger ever before—and I mean, ever before—has had such training as he had.

"But public sentiment is flowing the other way now. It's flowing back toward Milton Rawlins just like it once flowed away from him. The good people of Lowndes County know a liar when they hear one, and, gentlemen of the jury, I hope you do, too. If you are going to convict Milton Rawlins, then convict him on evidence!"

He shouted the last word for emphasis and slammed the defense table with his fist again. His voice suddenly dropped to a pitiful whine and said, "Oh, that nigger, that nigger. When you leave his testimony, the state has not a single prop to support its case. Let me repeat that. When you leave Alf Moore's testimony, the state has not a single prop to support its case!"

He looked around the courtroom as though looking for Moore, who, of course, was locked in his cell across the street.

"We have the murderer in custody. Alf Moore! He has been coddled and coached, protected and shielded by the very people who are sworn to uphold the laws of this grand state. Milton Rawlins has a proven alibi; Moore admits he was at the Carter house. Gentlemen, who do you believe killed those children?"

Cooper read several authorities on circumstantial evidence and then turned to the jury again. "This case is based solely on circumstantial evidence and the testimony of Carter and Moore. One of them, Mr. Carter, has feuded with the Rawlinses for years, and he has changed his testimony any number of times. His neighbors say they would not believe him under oath. The other, Alf Moore, is a self-confessed liar...Yes, a self-confessed liar! Gentlemen, the state has nothing more than a very weak case of circumstantial evidence against Milton Rawlins, certainly not enough for a conviction in this case. In fact, I would caution you about placing too much trust in this kind of evidence. Would you want your life to hang on circumstantial evidence and the testimony of two unreliable witnesses? Remember, Alf Moore is a self-confessed liar, and Mr. Carter's neighbors have testified that they would not believe him under oath."

For nearly three hours, Cooper analyzed and dissected and tried to disprove virtually everything the two men had said on the witness stand.

Finally, his list of legal points depleted, Cooper turned to outright pleading. The *Valdosta Times* called Cooper "a master in the art of pleading" and the *Macon Telegraph* said he possessed "a rare ability to sway opinion with nothing more than emotional words and outright pleading."

"I beg of you, gentlemen of the jury, do not convict an innocent man on the flimsy evidence you have heard here. Above all, do not take a man's life on such circumstantial nonsense. Show fairness and mercy to Milton Rawlins as you would want fairness and mercy shown to you at the throne of God."

At noon, his clothes hanging in a limp mass upon his large frame, Cooper stood at the rail in front of the jury and looked each of the jurors in the eye, one by one. His final plea was aimed at getting at least a mistrial. "Gentlemen, if there is one member of this jury who is not satisfied that Milton Rawlins is the murderer of the Carter children, you should stand by your convictions...today and forever! Don't give in to others! Be your own man! Stand up for the truth as you see it!"

As he sat down and mopped his brow, the judge called a recess. Solicitor Thomas would have his turn when court resumed in an hour and a half.

Many of the spectators, wanting to hear Solicitor Thomas' final words in the dramatic case, did not leave their seats for the noon meal. Instead, they talked about the chance of a mistrial and the highlights of the testimony they had heard. Some argued the case like lawyers, but there was general agreement that the solicitor's presentation would be well worth missing a meal.

The electric fans whirred during the recess and the solicitor did not ask to have them turned off while he addressed the jury.

Thomas methodically and relentlessly wove testimony and physical evidence together, creating a compelling case for conviction. He showed little emotion and seldom raised his voice above a conversational level. "Thomas went about building his case much like a mathematician explaining a complicated equation in the simplest terms," the *Macon Telegraph* reported.

He revisited every important point of testimony, naming the witness who said it and adding the names of those who supported it. He retraced ownership and possession of the gun and knife taken from Alf Moore's shanty.

Thomas tried to explain inconsistencies in testimony given by Carter and Moore. Carter, he said, did not name the McDonalds during the coroner's inquest at the crime scene for two reasons. First, the jurors there did not ask for a complete list of those at the scene, only who killed the children. Second, he said Carter, who had just endured a night of terror, knew the McDonalds were related to the sheriff at the scene and feared reprisal if he identified them at the time.

Moore, he said, delayed telling the entire story for two reasons. First, he was afraid he might get lynched if he told too much. Second, he was holding back some details so he might make a deal later with authorities—a deal that was never made, he emphasized.

He spoke just over an hour. By the time he finished, the afternoon heat in the courtroom was almost unbearable.

The judge then charged the jury and sent them out to decide Milton Rawlins' fate. As soon as the jury was gone, the judge told the packed courtroom that, while he would await the verdict on Milton Rawlins that evening, the court would conduct no new business until Monday when the next trial would begin.

At that point, Cooper made a motion that Leonard and Jesse Rawlins be tried together. A surprised Solicitor Thomas quickly agreed, saying it "would save a lot of time and money."

Cooper's reason for wanting to try the other two boys together was simple. In case of a conviction, a jury surely wouldn't sentence Leonard to hang for just being at the scene.

And if a jury recommended mercy for Leonard, then Jesse, just sixteen years old, stood a better chance of escaping the gallows.

"Lump them together and hope for the best," he told his partner, O.M. Smith, who at first seemed surprised by Cooper's sudden change of heart.

Cooper also made a motion for a continuance, saying it had been a long, hot week and he could use the time to recuperate physically and prepare for the joint trial, too. If he was hoping his agreeing to a joint trial might get a continuance, he was disappointed. The judge ruled against his motion.

As the judge left the courtroom, the Carters — mother, father and five surviving children including a baby in arms — left special seating near the judge's bench through a rear door and went to a room on the first floor to await the verdict. They seemed to have few friends and supporters.

At the banister separating spectators from court officials, Mrs. Rawlins and her daughters gathered to talk to Milton and Joe Rawlins. Interested parties encircled the group, and Mrs. Rawlins freely discussed her son's case, saying that the jury surely would acquit him. None of the Rawlinses "exhibited the least bit of nervousness," the *Macon Telegraph* reported. "To one not within earshot, it appeared to be just a gathering of friends."

One topic of conversation among the Rawlins family and their supporters was the cost of the trial. Joe Rawlins estimated the worth of his estate at about five thousand dollars and he said that sum would soon be "exhausted." Squire Jowers was present at that discussion but did not say anything about his own expenditures in the case.

After a while, conversations subsided and there seemed to be nothing to do but wait. The attorneys, who had finished their work for the day, drifted away to other rooms within the courthouse. Finally, only the two prisoners and four guards remained inside the banister, and the guards decided to escort the prisoners to the jail across the street. Few spectators chose to stay in the courtroom.

Mrs. Rawlins and her daughters went to their room at the Florence Hotel. On the street, a *Macon Telegraph* reporter described the scene this way: "The crowd was thick about the courthouse and...a very striking gathering beneath the electric lights (newly installed on the courthouse grounds). As the hours drew on, the crowd lessened, of course, but most spectators remained on the courthouse grounds and in the corridors until the verdict came in."

An impromptu survey on the streets by newspaper reporters showed that most spectators were leaning toward a mistrial, believing the jury was divided and that a unanimous verdict would prove impossible.

Finally, at half past eight o'clock, the judge received word that a verdict had been reached. His appearance let the spectators know that the verdict was in and, within minutes, the courtroom was filled to capacity again.

Milton Rawlins was quickly brought from the jail and, at 8:45, the jury entered the courtroom. For the first time since the trial began, no family member was at his side. Mrs. Rawlins and her daughters did not have time to come from the hotel before the verdict was read, and Milton's father was not given the option of returning to the courtroom for the verdict. The defendant sat at the defense table with only his attorneys.

The *Valdosta Times* said young Rawlins "evidently had retired for the night and wore his coat closely about his neck to hide the undershirt beneath it...and for the first time, he showed signs of the tremendous struggle which was being waged within his bosom." Milton sat "as stolid as a statue of marble," the *Times* reported. "His sharp features (were) perfectly rigid and his eyes followed the jurors as they moved into their seats."

The judge asked, "Gentlemen, have you agreed upon a verdict?"

"We have, your honor," said jury foreman W. H. Starling. Then he stood and handed the written verdict to the solicitor.

Thomas read aloud, "We, the jury, find the defendant guilty."

A tense silence gripped the courtroom spectators. They waited. Was that all?

No recommendation for mercy was made.

Judge Mitchell broke the heavy silence by saying, "Mr. Foreman, I would suggest that you make the verdict read, 'We, the jury, find the defendant, Milton Rawlins, guilty.'"

The change was quickly made, and the verdict was read again, this time including Milton's name.

Again, the spectators waited in tense silence.

No recommendation for mercy was forthcoming.

The prisoner would face the gallows.

Milton Rawlins showed no emotion when the verdict was read. Spectators accepted the verdict in complete silence.

Cooper broke the tense moment by asking to poll the jury. One by one, jury members stood and confirmed the verdict.

The judge said he would pass sentence at some later date. With that statement, the judge banged his gavel and left the bench.

Cooper turned to Milton. "We'll appeal. This is just the first step. I know you're innocent and I will prove it."

As the officers put handcuffs on the prisoner, he showed little emotion. He said to Cooper, "Tell Ma I want to see her."

He left the courtroom without showing any great emotion, but the *Times* reported that, once Milton reached his cell, "he wept like a child."

As the jurors left the courthouse, they talked with acquaintances, and it soon became common knowledge that most of the four hours spent in session by the jurors was not needed to decide guilt or innocence. That was accomplished in a matter of minutes, they said. The issue of clemency was debated for more than three hours.

14

July 22, 1905

ANGELINE RAWLINS WENT TO THE VALDES HOTEL ON SATUR-
day morning, hoping to talk to Cooper before she faced
Milton for the first time since the verdict. When she learned
the attorney had returned to Macon late Friday night, she
became upset. She was still in an agitated state half an hour
later when she located O.M. Smith at his home.

"I hope Mr. Cooper hasn't given up on the other trials," a
worried Angeline said. "We have money. We will pay for the
defense of the others."

Smith assured her that Cooper would be back on Sunday
night and would be ready for the second trial on Monday
morning. "He's still registered at the Valdes," Smith said.
"He'll be back. Believe me, we are not even close to giving up.
In fact, Mr. Cooper went to Macon to engage law students at
the Mercer University Law School to begin researching points
on circumstantial evidence for Milton's appeal. He has told
me he will stay with these cases to the very end. He's that
kind of lawyer, Mrs. Rawlins."

Satisfied with Smith's explanation, a tired and drawn
Angeline headed for the jail.

She needed to comfort her son.

Quite a large crowd had gathered outside the jail to
discuss the case and a *Times* reporter was in the midst of it,

scribbling notes for his next story. But silence quickly settled on the group when Angeline and her daughters appeared.

As she went inside to see the sheriff, the *Times* reporter followed her. The sheriff guided Mrs. Rawlins to a cell in the old part of the jail that was shared by Milton and his father. The reporter was allowed to follow and he reported this conversation:

Mrs. Rawlins: "I just came to tell you not to give up, Milton. We've got a lawyer who says he will stick with us to the end, and this trial is just the beginning. I just talked to Mr. Smith, and he said Mr. Cooper is in Macon right now getting some help with your appeal."

Milton: "I know there is a whole heap of folks around here in a worse fix than I am right now."

Joe Rawlins: "You're right, Milton. You are not in half as bad a fix as those folks who have lied about you. The Bible does not say that no murderer shall reach heaven, but it distinctly says that all liars shall be cast into outer darkness. You are as innocent of this crime as I am. I know I am innocent and I believe you are."

Mrs. Rawlins: "The very idea of anybody being able to identify anyone by moonlight is too foolish for anyone with common sense to even consider. Yet, those people swore they could and that they saw you."

Quiet filled the room and tears welled up in the mother's eyes.

Mrs. Rawlins: "The verdict was guilty and the jury didn't even give you mercy, Milton, so I guess that means they want to hang you."

The statement brought the girls to tears and Milton also wept.

Joe Rawlins paid no attention to the weeping girls. Instead, he raised his voice so he could be heard over the sobs. He was naturally a loud talker, and there had been an air of defiance about him since he'd been in jail.

Joe: "I feel this way. I would rather see this boy hung than to see him sent to the penitentiary for life."

Mrs. Rawlins: "Oh, no! Hanging is an awful thing!"

Joe: "I know it's an awful thing, but it is not as awful as an innocent man having to spend the rest of his life in a chain gang. Now, if Milton was guilty, I would rather he was sent to the penitentiary for life. I know I would if it was me. Then I would have time to reflect and get ready for the future. But if I was innocent, I would rather be hung and get through it. And that's just what I want for my boy. If they are determined to lay this crime on my son, then let them hang him and get it done. It is life and liberty, or it is death for me. It's the same for my son."

Mrs. Rawlins gave her husband a look that was meant to silence the kind of talk she'd just heard and then she turned to her son, "Well, Milton, they aren't going to hang you. You are suffering right now in this jail more than you will ever suffer in your life again. But you are not going to hang. There are higher courts than this one, and we are going all the way to the top!"

Before leaving the jail, Mrs. Rawlins said she might come back on Sunday, but her husband urged her to "stay at home and get rested" for the Monday session of court.

Joe also told his wife that she should "sell the good horse" to help pay legal fees "if you can get a good price...but don't sacrifice the animal" to cheap prices.

"That statement," reported The *Macon Telegraph*, "is almost like a tragedy itself. Within a few weeks, a once-prominent and well-to-do citizen, with handsome boys and pretty, rosy-cheeked girls, finds all of his possessions swept away in order that money might be had to defend him and his sons in a trial for their lives—for murder."

As Mrs. Rawlins left the cell, herding the whimpering girls in front of her, she said, "Now remember, Milton, don't give up. You'll come out of this all right."

Joe stood there with an arm around his son's shoulders and said, "Yes, we're going to be all right -- all of us. We have truth and right on our side. Even God is on our side. Hear that Milton? God is on our side!"

Milton managed a smile.

In Sunday's edition, the *Macon Telegraph* reported Leonard and Jesse Rawlins were on the verge of a breakdown. A confession and a plea for mercy might be forthcoming at any moment, the story said.

"The two boys, who are confined to the same cell, sent for Sheriff Passmore (on Saturday) and asked him what he thought they ought to do. The sheriff told them they ought to get that advice from their lawyer. But then the sheriff added, 'If I was guilty, I would say so, and if I was innocent, I would stick to it.'

"Then the boys asked the sheriff if he would talk to Alf Moore and find out what he was going to swear against them. Later in the afternoon, the sheriff talked to the Negro. He came back and told the boys Alf would swear that Jesse and Leonard were there (at the scene of the crime) and Jesse fired one of the shots. The Negro said, 'If Jesse and Leonard was not there, I was not there, Milton was not there and the old man didn't hire me...but they were sho' there.'

"When the boys were informed of what Moore said, Jesse replied, 'Well, well, what are we going to do now?' He paused a moment and said to the sheriff, "You know, I haven't said that Pa didn't hire that Negro.'

"The sheriff told them he was in a hurry and left the cell, but it looked very much like they wanted to release their burden by making a statement."

A copy of the newspaper relaying that incident reached Joe Rawlins' cell at midmorning and Joe immediately started hollering for the sheriff. "What the hell is going on, sheriff? Are you trying to get mixed up in this by giving advice to my boys about what they ought to do? My lawyer is going to have your ass in court, and we'll see what the judge has to say about this."

Sheriff Passmore spoke defiantly, "When anyone asks me a question, I try to give them an answer. Even the prisoners."

Rawlins, his face flushed with anger, said, "I wanna talk to my boys right now. You God-damned people–"

The sheriff interrupted him with, "You ain't gonna get much of anything talking like that."

"Well, let me see my boys," Rawlins said in a quieter tone. "And I'd like for my lawyer to come down here."

The sheriff delivered the boys to the cell a few minutes later and informed Rawlins that Cooper was out of town. "I called the hotel and they say he went back to Macon."

"Can you get Mr. Smith down here?"

"I'll see what I can do," the sheriff said.

Joe turned to the boys. "Ready to give up, huh?" he asked and jammed the newspaper into their hands.

The boys read the story and then adamantly stated they were not about to give up. "We was just trying to find out what he (Moore) was going to say against us, Pa," Jesse said.

"Well, I think you boys had better leave that to the lawyers and me," Joe said, "and you ought to keep your mouths shut. Didn't I tell you not to talk to anybody about anything?"

The boys, their heads hanging like sheep in a rainstorm, murmured, "Yes, sir."

John Randolph Cooper returned to Valdosta Sunday afternoon on the 6:10 train and went immediately to the Valdes Hotel. He had called Oscar Smith, his co-counsel, to meet him there.

Smith shook hands in the lobby and said, "Mrs. Rawlins was very upset when she learned that you weren't in town Saturday morning. And then old man Rawlins got upset when he found his boys were talking to the sheriff."

Cooper asked for details about the boys' conversation with the sheriff and then, handing his grip to a porter, headed directly to the jail.

He conferred with his clients for nearly an hour, reminded all of them of his previous advice to "keep a lid on it," and then walked to the street with Smith.

"My God, it's hot, Oscar. I don't know how much more of this I can take."

Smith nodded agreement. The weather was indeed scorching hot. "I don't know why the judge ever picked a month like this to have a special session."

"To expedite justice, Oscar. Why else?"

As they reached the hotel door and found a cool spot beneath an electric fan, Cooper told his partner, "Same courtroom, same testimony, different jury. I wish we had a different judge, too. You know, I talked to a couple of friends in Macon who are law professors. They agreed with me that Moore's testimony should not have been allowed. We're going to jump on him hard the next time he gets on the stand."

They talked strategy until after midnight. When Smith finally left, Cooper walked to the lobby with him. A light rain was falling outside and the temperature was coming down quickly.

"Looks like the morning will be bearable," Cooper said.

Smith nodded, jammed his hat on and walked out into the rain.

The crowd for the second trial was only a fraction of what it had been the previous week. Two factors contributed to the decrease. First, spectators expected to hear a replay of testimony from the first trial and, second, jury selection on that first day was regarded as a very boring process. A few seats were still available when the session began.

As soon as Judge Mitchell brought order to the courtroom, Cooper immediately asked for a change of venue. He cited the same basic reason as before—an inflamed public mind. Then he added one more: excessive publicity.

"Everybody in every part of this county knows every detail of the Milton Rawlins trial," Cooper contended. "They (the newspapers) are getting out issues every few minutes, telling everything that is said. A witness hardly gets off the stand before newsboys are selling newspapers telling what he said. I repeat that, in view of such intense publicity, we ought to have a change of venue."

The attorney sat down and almost immediately stood up again. "I don't mean that the papers have been unfair to my clients. Much of what they have said has been in favor of the accused. I was simply referring to the great amount of publicity this case has been given."

The motion was denied.

With motions out of the way, the trial picked up steam. Cooper asked for Joe Rawlins' presence in the courtroom to assist in jury selection. The judge agreed.

Mrs. Rawlins and the boys' sisters were also in the courtroom, sitting in the first row of public seating behind the defense table.

A story by the *Valdosta Times* drew a graphic word-picture of the Rawlins family:

> Jesse and Leonard Rawlins sat without showing any emotion. Both of them are good-looking boys, and Jesse has a dreamy, sleepy look that is not unbecoming. Leonard is very light complected (sic); his hair is a sandy color. Neither boy looks like he could have been induced to commit the crime with which they are charged.
>
> Their two sisters and mother were with them in the courtroom. The girls were eating candy from a bag, and they passed it down the line. Each of the boys and the old man took some and ate it.
>
> Mrs. Rawlins presented a pitiful picture. There was a despondent, worn, listless look upon her face. Deep lines of sorrow were written around her eyes, and grief too great for tears was chiseled upon her general expression. She paid little attention to what was going

on, but it was evident that she felt that the fate of Milton would also come to her other two boys.

Rawlins—the old man—appeared a little bit nervous, but not much more than other occasions since the trials began.

The *Macon Telegraph* offered this account:

The mother seems to be the only one who has lost hope. She appears utterly hopeless. Her grief is shown in every line on her face, and is touching to the stoutest heart.

A jury was seated by two o'clock and, as soon as witnesses were sworn, testimony began.

W. L. Carter again told his account of the night of terror when his two children were killed. He was just as emphatic as before that he was looking at his children when they were shot and that he could identify those who did the shooting. He also repeated—over objections by Cooper—that his dying son said Jesse shot him and Milton killed his sister. He also identified Leonard as being at the scene but not taking part in the killings.

On cross-examination, Cooper, speaking calmly and exhibiting none of the dramatics accompanying his first encounter with Carter, questioned him on the same points. Why didn't he tell the coroner's jury Leonard was there? Why didn't he tell the coroner's jury that he saw Jim and Tim McDonald at the scene? Did he ever suggest that one of the men at the scene had a "smutty face"? Was his son really lucid at the time he told who shot him?

Cooper also questioned Carter at length about problems he'd had with neighbors. And he alluded to the large sums of money Carter kept in his house and suggested that "robbery by Alf Moore and his henchmen was the real motive" for the assault on Carter's house.

Cooper's cross-examination of Carter in the second trial wasn't nearly as "hard-boiled" or as "cruel" as the first interrogation, news reports said. However, Cooper, under a strategy in which the defense would put no witnesses on the stand later, attacked Carter's character with questions rather than using testimony of defense witnesses later.

Cooper: "Didn't they prosecute you and run you out of the county from which you came when you moved to Lowndes County?"

Carter: "I'm not compelled to answer that question, but I will do so. No, they did not."

Cooper: "Didn't they get a warrant for you for forging land deeds?"

Carter: "No, sir, there was no warrant against me and never a judgment against me. I owe no man an honest dollar."

Cooper: "Didn't they stop you from preaching at Hahira?"

Carter: "They did not. I withdrew my application."

Seeming satisfied that he had planted seeds of doubt in the jurors' minds, Cooper abruptly said, "No more questions," and sat down.

Alf Moore took the stand next and, as he told his story under the orchestration of the solicitor, Cooper "watched the witness like a hawk sizing up its prey," the *Macon Telegraph* reported. Moore's account was nearly an exact duplicate of the story he told in the Milton Rawlins trial, and he was interrupted a dozen times as Cooper raised objections to the admissibility of what he was saying. Each time the judge overruled him.

This second telling brought out a few more details, and at least one illustrated the father's dominance of his sons. Moore gave a more detailed account of the meeting in the shanty on the afternoon before the killings. He quoted Joe Rawlins as saying to Milton, "I want this done and done right." Milton replied, "I'll do the best I can." Moore said the elder Rawlins raised his voice, punched a finger against his son's chest and said, "I don't want the best you can do. I want this thing done right. I am not to be tried, nor hung. Don't tell me you're going to do the best you can. Say you're just going to do the God-damned thing right!"

Milton said, "Yes, sir, Pa, I'll do it right."

Moore added, "Them boys follered Mr. Rawlins around like a bunch of puppies and did everything he said."

Judge Mitchell called a halt to the trial at half past six, saying Alf Moore would resume his testimony at eight o'clock Tuesday morning.

15

SOON AFTER TUESDAY'S SESSION COMMENCED, COOPER GOT HIS chance to break down Moore's testimony. He questioned Moore about his arrest record, the difference in his stories at the time of his arrest and on the witness stand, and if he had had any "training" by the prosecution. Cooper's questions, regardless of the answers, were meant to discredit him before the jurors.

Cooper's grilling of the witness was intense but lasted less than half an hour. Then the same witnesses who had testified in the first trial paraded to the stand, told essentially the same stories and were asked the same questions under cross-examination.

The state rested its case before noon, and the judge was ready to start hearing defense witnesses. But Cooper made a surprise request. He wanted a recess, he said, so he could consult with his colleagues and clients, adding that perhaps he could "shorten this trial considerably."

His request fueled speculation that the boys might be ready to plead guilty and beg for mercy.

As the courtroom was emptying, Joe Rawlins said he was "mighty sick," and asked to see a doctor. He was returned to the jail and a doctor dispatched to attend to him.

When court resumed at 1:30 P.M., Leonard Rawlins took the stand and made an unsworn statement. (In making an unsworn statement, a defendant takes no oath and may say anything that could aid the defense—without fear of cross-examination.)

Leonard said he and his brothers were innocent, that Moore had lied from beginning to end, and that Carter was mistaken in identifying him and his brothers as being among the attackers at his house on the night of the murders.

Jesse followed and said almost exactly the same thing.

Neither of the boys' statements lasted more than ten minutes.

Cooper then surprised the state by announcing that the defense would call no witnesses. This maneuver, by rules governing the practice of law, gives the defense the advantage of making the last—and hopefully the most impressionable—argument to the jury.

Solicitor Thomas, obviously miffed by the tactic, called Deputy Crosby to the stand and attempted to show that Cooper had subpoenaed witnesses who could offer testimony beneficial to the defense of the accused.

Judge Mitchell said Cooper was free to conduct his defense as he saw fit, and that final arguments would begin.

Whitaker and Smith, assistants on opposite sides of the case, offered nothing unusual in their presentations, choosing to explain evidence and try to tie it together. By the time Whitaker finished, it was six o'clock, and Judge Mitchell banged his gavel and called it a day.

On Wednesday morning, solicitor Thomas spent an hour and fifty minutes once again weaving testimony and evidence into a tight web around the accused boys. That finished, he referred to an appeal made the previous evening by defense attorney Smith in which Smith had asked the jury to show mercy for the "minor boys" on trial.

"What kind of mercy did the minor children of W.L. Carter get?" the solicitor asked with a bit of sarcasm. "They were shot down in cold blood. If we're going to talk about 'minor children,' let's talk about the Carter children, too."

He declared that a clearer case for conviction—and hanging—"never has been laid out in any courtroom." He asked for murder convictions against both Rawlins boys.

Attorney Cooper, having the last word with the jury, gave one of the great performances in his fifteen years of practicing law. For two hours and a half, he picked apart the state's case. The state, he said, had nothing but circumstantial evidence and a man's life should never be taken on such tentative— and sometimes unreliable—information.

He also said the state made a great case of innocence for the Rawlins boys, and that Alf Moore did the killing to steal Carter's money. And he told the jurors that, if they sent the boys to their deaths, they surely would live to regret it.

In concluding his speech, Cooper told the jurors that if they found the boys guilty, they should show mercy. And then he began to paint what he called "the saddest picture I've ever seen, one that will stay with me the rest of my life."

"Just thirty-some days ago," he said in a most dramatic tone, "a citizen of this county, J.G. Rawlins, was happy in his home with his family about him. He had everything a man could want. Now he is sick and in prison. His eldest son has been condemned to die on the gallows. His youngest son—whom fathers love the most—and the next one are on trial here. The old mother and her daughters are desolate and hopeless in the shadow of this great sorrow that has come upon their lives."

The *Macon Telegraph* gave this account: "As the lawyer described the situation, the Rawlins boys wiped tears from their eyes, and their mother and sisters buried their faces and wept. Tears streamed down the face of the attorney as he spoke. Even the jurors seemed visibly affected by the pathetic picture he painted.

"The attorney again begged the jury to show mercy as they would have mercy shown to them. And he said if there was one man who favored acquittal, he hoped that man would hold out for all times."

Judge Mitchell charged the jury just before noon and sent it behind closed doors to decide the fate of the two younger Rawlins' boys. And the jurors went without lunch, the *Valdosta Times* reported. Undoubtedly, the judge expected a quick verdict, but deliberations dragged on for four hours. Finally, word came that a verdict had been reached.

Jesse and Leonard entered the courtroom just before five o'clock. They were chained together and "entered the courtroom in a swaggering glide, came down the aisle and took seats reserved for them," news reports said. The judge then admonished spectators packed into the courtroom against any outburst or demonstration.

The *Macon Telegraph* recorded the dramatic scene this way:

> When the jury came out, there was breathless stillness in the room and a solemn feeling prevailed as the judge asked if a verdict had been reached. Solicitor Thomas stepped forward and received the verdict from jury foreman B.H. Jones. And he read slowly, 'We, the jury, find the defendants, Leonard Rawlins and Jesse Rawlins, guilty of murder, and recommend that Leonard Rawlins be sent to the penitentiary for life.'
>
> The mother of the boys broke down and cried like a child.
>
> Attorney Cooper then asked that a poll of the jury be taken. As the names of the jurors were called, each rose and acknowledged the verdict.
>
> The verdict seemed to lift the burden from Leonard Rawlins, but it only added to the strain under which Jesse was struggling.

Again, the judge said he would delay sentencing until later, and the boys were returned to their cell.

Solicitor Thomas then said he wanted to start the trial of Joe Rawlins the next morning. Cooper immediately made a motion for a delay, saying the elder Rawlins was sick in his cell and physicians were attending him.

The judge looked to Thomas for an answer and the solicitor said Alf Moore would be tried on Thursday morning. The solicitor noted that Moore did not have an attorney, and Judge Mitchell appointed three—J.G. Cranford, A.T. Woodard and C.L. Smith.

Meanwhile, the judge instructed the sheriff to report to him the next morning on the condition of Joe Rawlins.

Just before seven o'clock on Thursday morning, Moore was brought into the courtroom and taken to a room where his newly appointed attorneys waited. After just an hour of consultations, the lawyer, the prisoner and two guards moved into the courtroom for the trial.

The courtroom was less than half filled with spectators, and most of those were other black people seated in the balcony.

The same string of witnesses—with the exception of Moore himself—took the stand and repeated testimony they had given during the trials of the Rawlins boys. When Moore was called to the stand, he told the same story he had been telling. He asked for mercy for himself—"and with equal earnestness," according to the *Valdosta Times*—asked for mercy for all of the Rawlins boys as well. He said Joe Rawlins instigated the whole affair and ordered his sons into the fray. He admitted agreeing to help kill the family for a hundred dollars, noting that he and Leonard played similar roles in the attack—both were there but neither fired a gun. Then he begged for mercy one more time and stepped down from the witness stand.

The defense attorneys said since the defendant had voluntarily confessed his part in the crime, there was little need to call witnesses. Moore had left nothing unsaid, so the defense would simply rest its case.

The solicitor, in lieu of a closing statement, read the law that had been broken, the punishment prescribed and again clearly stated the facts of the case. Then he sat down, seemingly unsure about how the case was being conducted.

Cranford made the closing statement for the defense, noting that Moore had confessed, aided the state's case in two previous trials and did not kill anyone. In fact, he pointed out, Moore surely saved Mrs. Carter's life when the attackers first arrived at the house. He begged for clemency for his client.

The trial phase lasted four hours. The judge charged the jury and took a recess until 1:30 P.M.

By the time court resumed, a verdict was ready. The prisoner was brought back to the courtroom. As soon as the jury was seated, foreman J. P. Coffee rose and handed the written verdict to Thomas, who read: "We, the jury, find the defendant, Alf Moore, guilty of murder."

There was no recommendation for mercy.

Moore said to Cranford, "I thought they would show mercy after all I done."

"We'll try to work that out," Cranford said as Moore was hurried back to the jail.

The state immediately called for the trial of Joe Rawlins to begin. Before Cooper could rise to make a motion, the judge asked, "Mister Sheriff, is the prisoner in the court?"

"No, sir, but I can have him here in just a minute."

"Let him be brought in."

Cooper then made a motion for a continuance, saying the defendant was "too sick to go to trial."

Meanwhile, the sheriff rushed to the jail and found Rawlins reclining on a cot. Saying he was too sick to go to trial, he refused to leave the jail.

When the sheriff reported back, Judge Mitchell, who had ordered a physical checkup by two physicians earlier in the day, then told the sheriff to bring Rawlins to the courtroom, "even if he has to be carried on a cot."

In a short while, Rawlins appeared, hobbling slowly along between two deputies "as though he was nearly dead," according to the *Macon Telegraph*.

The physicians who had examined him earlier testified that the only thing wrong with Rawlins was a painful fissure of the anus, a condition that he had had for some time. He also had a case of nervousness which, they noted, "is to be expected."

Dr. B. S. Burton testified the prisoner's "vital signs are normal—temperature, pulse, respiration—and there is no internal organ, no vital organ, affected except his rectum. It is especially inflamed today...and he may have a difficult time sitting for prolonged periods of time."

The judge thanked the physicians and then ordered that a cot be brought into the courtroom. He said he would allow Rawlins to recline on the cot if the prisoner did not feel like sitting up.

The sheriff took the stand and noted that Rawlins had been in court every day—until it was his turn to be tried.

The judge overruled the motion for a continuance.

Cooper then offered a motion for a continuance because of his own physical condition, saying he was "worked down" because of two highly charged, back-to-back trials during "the hottest two weeks I've ever known." Besides, he said, he had caught an awful cold and he needed the rest.

Judge Mitchell praised Cooper as having been "as active as any member of the bar ever had been, maybe even more so." Then he overruled that motion, too.

Those proceedings—motions by Cooper and just getting Rawlins into court—had consumed the afternoon. As the hour of six o'clock approached, Judge Mitchell gaveled the session to an end, saying jury selection would begin Friday morning.

As deputies put handcuffs on Rawlins for the walk back to the jail, he told Cooper, "We need to talk tonight."

Cooper nodded and followed the party across the street to the jail. Smith walked with him.

"He's pretty shaken," Smith observed.

"Yeah, we need a good performance from him tomorrow," Cooper said. "Let's get him pumped up."

In the jail, Cooper told Rawlins, "We're going the same way with you as we did with the boys—no witnesses. That'll give us the final say to the jury."

"I don't know," Rawlins said. "It didn't work last time."

"Yes," Cooper said, "but this time we have you making that unsworn statement. You know the state's witnesses and you can do more to help the case than putting your wife and daughters and your friends on the stand. The first jury didn't believe them, and I don't think this one will, either."

Milton, who was in the cell, said, "I think Mr. Cooper is right, Pa. You brought up a lot of good points at my trial."

The old man looked at his son proudly. "You like the old man's work, huh?"

Milton nodded.

Joe turned back at the attorneys and said, "OK, we'll do it your way."

Cooper pulled out a list of witnesses and said, "You're going to have a lot of rebuttal to do. And we've got a couple of witnesses we haven't seen before. Who is S. S. Kemp?"

"Methodist preacher," Joe answered. "A friend of Carter's."

"What is he going to say?"

Joe shrugged. "Beats me."

"You ever do him any wrong?"

"Not that I recall."

"Noah Tyler?"

"Another preacher."

Cooper asked questions for half an hour and then turned to leave. "Be at your best tomorrow," he said to Rawlins. "We may get to you before the day is over. Eat a good meal and get some rest. I don't want to see your head resting on a satchel tomorrow. I want you ready to go."

"Yes, sir," Rawlins said.

16

AFTER TWO WEEKS OF HIGHLY CONTESTED TESTIMONY IN TWO Rawlins trials, the people who followed the proceedings were going to get what they wanted most—the trial of the father who stood accused of instigating the whole affair. The general consensus was that Joe Rawlins would eventually take the stand in his own defense, and for many of the onlookers this would be the climax to a riveting two weeks.

The other trials generated much interest, but in the end, only raised more disturbing questions. Had Joe Rawlins really sent his teen-age sons on a killing rampage? If so, what motivated a man to do something like that? Why, people asked, had none of the three boys refused to follow his orders to wipe out an entire family?

The *Valdosta Times* reported the largest crowd for any trial ever held in Valdosta. Restaurants once again advertised "twenty-four hour service until the end of the trial." The signs didn't say the Joe Rawlins trial, just THE trial.

Reporters again converged on the farm community near the Florida line. Street vendors hawked cold drinks and frilly umbrellas intended for ladies' protection from the blistering rays of the summer sun. In the courthouse, deputies worked to keep hallways from getting clogged, and Sheriff Passmore was once again busy assigning seats and trying to keep order in the courtroom.

The weather was reminiscent of the first few days of Milton's trial, and only the electric fans kept a small breeze moving in the courtroom. Everyone dreaded the stifling heat of the coming days, but the excitement of the moment, the chance to be in the midst of it all, far outweighed the discomfort.

One man who was conspicuous by his absence at Joe's trial was Squire Jowers. The grandfather of the boys was finally convinced that Passmore was right, that Joe Rawlins was indeed guilty. He was at the train station when a *Valdosta Times* reporter approached him and, noting that his son-in-law had said he was nearly broke, asked if Jowers was going to pay for Joe Rawlins' defense.

Jowers crustily replied, "I will try to help my grandboys out of this jam, but I wouldn't give one kopeck (a foreign coin worth a fraction of an American cent) to save Joe Rawlins' hide."

When Angeline saw that quote in the paper, she became upset, but her father had already returned to Coffee County. Angeline's brother, Gene, who had sat through most of the first two trials, also left immediately after the verdict in the second trial.

As jury selection began, Joe Rawlins, appearing in much better health than the previous day, half lay and half sat on his cot as attorney Cooper put the prospective jurors through rigid examination. The attorney's obvious strategy was to make still another appeal for a change of venue by centering his questions on the unprecedented publicity given the earlier trials.

"Have you read the newspapers?" he asked one prospect after another.

Every would-be juror answered in the affirmative.

"Have you read about this case."

Invariably, that brought a "Yes, sir."

"Have you formed an opinion about this case?"

The prospects split on that point. Some admitted having formed an opinion; some said they had not. Most who admitted to having an opinion about the case said they believed the previous verdicts were correct, that the Rawlins boys were guilty.

Cooper then told the court that newspaper accounts on the case had been both intense and accurate and, because of that, people had ample opportunity to form opinions about the case. He said that anyone who had formed an opinion should not be seated on the jury. The judge agreed, disqualifying a large number of prospects. The decision saved time because Cooper would not have to weed out biased prospects.

The defense attorney subjected those who remained to another string of rapid-fire questions. And Rawlins, although he sometimes reclined on his cot, proved once again to be helpful since he knew the lines of friendship and allegiance in much of the county.

At 11:30, the twelfth juror was seated and, after the state's witnesses were sworn, Solicitor Thomas told the jury what to expect from the prosecution's witnesses.

"The details of this crime will stagger your imagination," he said. "We will present testimony to show that a fiendish desire has long lingered in the heart of Joe Rawlins to slay the entire Carter family."

At that statement, Rawlins, who had been in a semi-prone position on his cot, sat upright and fixed his gaze on the speaker's face until the conclusion of Thomas' remarks.

A recess was then taken until 1:30.

W.L. Carter again led off the state's case and told his story almost exactly like the other times. Because the story had been told and retold, some seats in the courtroom were empty at the start of the afternoon session. But the crowd in the downtown area diminished only slightly. Many spectators simply sought refuge in cooler places than the courtroom during phases of the trial they considered less interesting.

Carter finished his account of the murders in about twenty-five minutes, but cross-examination lasted more than an hour. Cooper challenged Carter on the same points of testimony as before. Didn't he tell Sheriff Passmore that

Leonard might as well be released because the boy was not there? Did he really get around well enough to be standing on the back porch of the house when the shots were fired or was he relegated almost constantly to a prone position? Could he really identify men only by moonlight as they stood in the shade of a peach tree more than twenty paces away? Did he see Jim and Tim McDonald at his place about 10:00 P.M.? Or was it 1:00 A.M.? Or did he really see them at all? And why didn't he tell the sheriff they were there?

Cooper's questions, regardless of the answers Carter gave, were intended to sow doubt in the minds of the jurors.

Surprisingly, Cooper made no attack on Carter's character as he had done in the first trial with witnesses and in the second with a suggestive line of questioning.

Alf Moore again followed Carter to the witness stand. Solicitor Thomas obviously wanted to mesh Moore's testimony with Carter's story while it was still fresh in the minds of the jurors.

Moore's conviction and the lack of a recommendation for mercy seemed to have no affect on his testimony. He told almost an exact duplicate of his previous accounts. Even though he told the story with less hesitation and fewer interruptions from the defense attorney than before, he consumed more than an hour before Thomas looked at Cooper and said, "Your witness, counselor."

Cooper immediately sought to bring out the conditions under which Moore first told the officers and his employer, E.L. Ivey, what he knew about the killings. Moore again quoted Ivey, owner of the cross-tie camp, as saying, "If I had fooled around and not let the officers get me, I might have been lynched. And he said now that the officers have got me, I ought to tell the truth." He again confirmed that Passmore and Crosby, with guns in their hands, were present and standing over him when Ivey told him he ought to tell the truth.

At that point, Cooper turned to the judge and said, "Your honor, the testimony of this witness was not freely and..." But Judge Mitchell cut him short. He held up a hand to silence Cooper and then said, "I have already ruled on the admissibility of this testimony, Mr. Cooper. Proceed with your questions for this witness."

Cooper questioned Moore relentlessly on every discrepancy between his testimony on the stand and his earlier confessions at Staunton and in the jail. Moore gave the same reasons as before—that he didn't want to get "murdered up" by telling too much before he was safely in jail.

He also denied—again—that anyone had been "schooling" him about what to say on the witness stand.

But he also made one startling statement. "I couldn't say exactly which one of the boys killed little Carrie Carter. Both of them shot at her. Milton shot both times. He killed Willie Carter. I don't know which one killed Carrie."

That differed from the dying statement of Willie Carter who said Jesse shot him, and Cooper hammered home that point, making sure every juror knew about that conflict in the testimony by Moore and Carter.

After grilling Moore for more than an hour, Cooper finished up the cross-examination with questions of his own: "You admit you lied to officers soon after your arrest? You admit you didn't tell the truth when you first confessed in jail? Then why should these jurors believe you now?"

Moore shrugged his shoulders and said, "Well, I'm telling the truth now."

Ella Carter and her daughter, Lora, followed Moore and repeated their earlier accounts. Mrs. Carter was on the stand only about ten minutes and Lora for less than half an hour. Cooper chose not to aggressively cross-examine them. He was especially gentlemanly toward Lora, no doubt recalling her earlier admonition for his angry outburst in the first trial.

Ivey, the owner of the cross-tie camp, told essentially the same story as before, identifying the gun and knife as being the items he found in Moore's shanty in Staunton.

On cross-examination, he again testified that Moore was handcuffed and the two lawmen were there with guns in their hands when Ivey told Moore that "it would be better for him if he told the truth." Ivey also testified, "He told me the Rawlins boys were with him and that Mr. Rawlins hired him to kill the Carters for a hundred dollars."

"He said that up there at your commissary?"

"Yes, sir, he did."

Ivey said Moore told him a story with several differences when he talked to him in the jail a few days later.

Cooper: "So he lied to you twice?"

Ivey: "He changed what he said. Yes."

Cooper: "He lied to you twice?"

Ivey: "He changed parts of it both times. Yes, sir."

Fifteen-year-old Jim McDonald, and neighbors W.E. Martin and J.A. Stubbs repeated their earlier testimony about the knife swap and threats Rawlins made toward Carter. Martin testified that he'd heard so many threats against Carter's life "that it got to the point that I didn't pay much attention to them anymore."

Martin also quoted Rawlins as saying, "Guns may shoot, smoke and fire may boil up, women and children may scream, but you must turn your back, stay away from there (Carter's house)."

The courtroom was packed by the time the state introduced witnesses who had not appeared in the previous trials. Continuing to document threats Rawlins made toward Carter, two preachers were called to the stand.

S.S. Kemp, a Methodist minister, said he knew both Carter and Rawlins, and he had once tried to broker a peace between them. He said Carter, a member of his church, seemed willing to make peace. "But Mr. Rawlins said he would not make any compromise—or friendship—with Carter under any circumstances. He said he heard that Mr. Carter was taking out a peace warrant on him. Mr. Rawlins said, 'If he does, it will disarm me (those under peace bonds by law could not carry guns) so far as acting in the open is concerned. But I will get him if I have to crawl on my stomach to his place and lay around all night. A peace warrant will force me to act in the dark, but I will avenge myself. I will kill Carter'."

Kemp described himself as "a great friend to Carter," saying Carter "had lost his church membership, lost his credentials to preach, and was living in sin when I found him." He said he brought Carter back into the church but did not try to help him get his ministerial credentials restored.

Noah Tyler, a Baptist preacher, was the next witness. He described himself as a friend to both Carter and Rawlins and testified that he, too, tried to make peace between the two men.

"Mr. Rawlins didn't even want to talk about it (making peace)," Tyler said. "He said Carter was trying to put his boys under a peace bond. If he did that, Mr. Rawlins said, he would kill Carter if he had to crawl from his house to Carter's and shoot him through the cracks as he sat at his fireside."

Joe Gaddy, a farm hand who worked for Rawlins for several months immediately before the killings, was another new witness for the prosecution. He testified, "Mr. Rawlins came to me and said, 'Gaddy, if you tell me how to get out of this trouble and stay out of it, I will give you the finest suit of clothes that can be bought in Valdosta.'

"Mr. Rawlins said, 'The onliest way I can get out of it is to kill Carter, and it wouldn't do no good to kill him and leave the rest of the family here to worry me with the law as long as I live.' I also heard him tell Frank Turner that Carter wouldn't live to see the next frost fall."

Under cross-examination, he said Rawlins did not try to get him to kill Carter, just show him a way out of the trouble.

Lee Fiveash, a friend of the Rawlins family who had been a defense witness in Milton's trial, was the next witness. The solicitor asked him to repeat a statement he made in the first trial.

"Mr. Rawlins said he had a mind to kill old Carter and didn't believe it would be a sin in the sight of God to kill a man such as Carter."

J. F. Dasher, a neighbor testifying for the first time, told the court, "Mr. Rawlins told me that he would not swear that he would not spill Carter's blood."

Ella Jones again testified, "He (Rawlins) said that before Carter would be allowed to stay there, he would go and kill them from the baby up."

As she was excused from the stand, the clock in the tower struck eight o'clock. Judge Mitchell called a halt to the proceedings until eight o'clock Saturday morning.

As the deputies came to get Rawlins, Cooper, who had maintained a cordial relationship with the lawmen, held up his hand and said, "Give us just a minute."

The deputies stepped back and Cooper gave Rawlins a hard look. "How come you didn't tell me you conveyed threats to these preachers? Do you know the kind of weight their testimony will have with the jury?"

Joe's head dropped, his shoulders sagged and he said, "Sorry. I had no idea they were going to get on the stand and tell those lies."

"I really don't think the jury sees them as liars."

A tense silence fell between the two men.

"Do you have any more surprises for me?"

Joe shook his head and said, "My God, I hope not."

Cooper said, "I'm hoping not, too. Now get some rest. You're going to be on the stand tomorrow."

Then he motioned to the deputies to take his client back to jail.

17

WORD QUICKLY SPREAD THAT JOE BENTLEY, ONE OF THREE black men held in the killings, would testify first on Saturday, and the courtroom was filled to capacity an hour before the session began. The general consensus was that Bentley would be an interesting interlude while they waited to hear what Joe Rawlins might say.

Bentley testified that, on two occasions, Rawlins offered him a hundred dollars to kill Carter. "I told him, 'I can't do that; I don't have the grit'," the witness said. "Mr. Rawlins wanted to know if I knew someone who would do it. I told him I would ask around. But I didn't."

Bentley also said, "I ain't never been to the Carter house. I wasn't there the night of the killings. I was at home, sitting up with a sick child."

Mitch Johnson, the next witness, said he hauled cross-ties for E.L. Ivey and took a load to Hahira about a week before the children were killed. He said he met Joe Rawlins on the street and Rawlins took him aside and offered him a hundred dollars to kill Carter. When Johnson said he wouldn't do it, Rawlins asked if he knew the whereabouts of Alf Moore.

"I told him Alf was in Staunton," Johnson testified. "He didn't ask me anything else, and I left him there as politely as I could. When I got back to Staunton, I told Mr. Ivey that Rawlins had offered me a hundred dollars to kill Carter and, when I turned him down, he asked for Alf Moore."

Johnson denied any role in the killings, saying he never had been to the Carter house, either. "I know where it is. I could find it. But I ain't never been there."

At that point, Cooper asked that the testimony of Kemp, Tyler, Johnson and Turner be ruled out because Carter was not killed. Judge Mitchell overruled the motion.

The state offered just four more witnesses—bank teller J.Y. Blitch, hack driver Robert Dye, deputy sheriff J.F. Crosby and Hahira merchant C. W. Webb—who repeated testimony given in the earlier trials. There was little cross-examination.

The state then placed in evidence the guilty verdicts against the other four defendants as well as the peace bond for twelve hundred dollars against Joe Rawlins and the bill of indictment for the previous shotgun assault on W.L. Carter. Those documents were meant to support the state's case for accessory to murder.

Cooper objected to the introduction of the documents, but again he was overruled.

The state rested its case.

Spectators buzzed as Cooper called on the defendant to make an unsworn statement. That decision told the crowd the defense would once again offer no witnesses in order to get the final argument before the jury.

Joe Rawlins, described by the *Valdosta Times* as "a pathetic sight," moved slowly to the witness stand, eased carefully into the chair and then raised his gaze to the jurors seated a few paces away. In a low, pain-filled voice, he began to speak.

"Gentlemen of the jury, I am weak, sick in jail and not able to talk like I commonly talk, but I will try to talk so you can understand me.

"I am on trial for what is dearer to any man than anything else—his life. My satisfaction and happiness with my family and my property...gentlemen, that is all gone. I speak to you now, not to arouse your sympathy, but simply to state the facts of this case as I see them. I am a poor man, have been all my life. I was raised poor, but I tried to be honest. I don't think you can find any stain on my reputation up to the time this terrible tragedy occurred—a tragedy I know nothing about.

"I am not a man of fame. I worked hard and lived honest, and I tried to raise my family to work hard and live honest. I had some trouble with this man Carter, but nothing to warrant such a deed as has been committed out there."

Rawlins, warming to his task and gaining in volume, learned forward and in an earnest voice said, "Gentlemen of the jury, I wish—Oh, I would wish to the Almighty God—that the truth of this tragedy could be scrawled on the walls of this great temple of justice. Scrawl it in large letters so the whole world could read the truth as it exists. That is my heart's desire."

Rawlins then picked up a sheet of paper he had brought with him to the stand, lowered his voice a bit and said, "I made a few notes...because I knew I couldn't think of everything I wanted to say to you gentlemen."

"I came to Valdosta on that Tuesday, and I can prove I was here. I had legal business and I stayed here overnight."

Then Rawlins related his version of events on the day the children were killed and the day after.

"Mr. Stubbs is my friend. So is Ben Rice. We were together on Monday night before the tragedy. They quoted me as saying if old man Carter was killed that night, somebody would say it was me that done it. The reason I made that statement was because Ben Rice was talking about some trouble he and Carter had a year or two before that. Carter attacked his boy on the road and cursed him, and there was trouble between them.

"Ben said he went down to Carter's place with a gun and Carter came out with a gun and they had some words. He said he told Mr. Carter that if he had any more trouble with him, he would kill him. That's when I said, 'Yes, but if Carter was killed tonight, it wouldn't be laid to you. It would be laid to me.'

"Me and Carter had some trouble. It was the talk of the county and it was the talk of the town, and that is why I made that statement to Ben Rice."

In an appealing voice, Rawlins added, "Gentlemen, don't you know that if I had any idea of doing such a bloody deed as was done out there, why, I would never have made a remark such as that?"

He waited a moment, then he continued.

"Before I left Ben Rice's place, we had an agreement...that all three of us would come to Valdosta together on Tuesday morning. Well, I waited 'til dinnertime (noon) and then I gave up waiting on them. It was hot and dry, and I thought about going fishing down at the river. But a letter had come in the mail telling me the sheriff had some business with me. So I drove to Hahira and caught the train down here.

"When I was hitched up and ready to go, I put a watermelon in the buggy for Frank Turner, an old Negro who has been putting a chimney in my new house. He'd said he wanted a watermelon for his children. I took it and left it for him at Charlie Webb's store. Then I caught the train to Valdosta.

"I went to the bank to borrow some money to build a house on my place in Coffee County, but the teller said I would have to come back the next morning. That's what I wanted the money for. You can ask anybody who really knows me. I've been talking about building a house there for a couple of years, and I was finally going to start it."

He told about hearing the news of the killings the next morning, how he was arrested and bonded out on the assault charge. He recalled that by the time he was out of jail, the eleven o'clock train to Hahira had left. He hired a hack to carry him to his home. His story wound through the day's events—his arrest by Crosby, the search of his house for weapons, his eventual release at the Carter house and then his arrest the following morning in Valdosta.

Having explained his movements to his satisfaction, Rawlins told the jury he wanted to talk to them about the state's witnesses.

He started with Alf Moore's testimony, saying that everything the witness had said—from where they met, the crops that were planted in the fields, a tree stump that really wasn't there, the kind of fence around his place—was false. He described his place and told how it differed with Moore's testimony. "I'm not sure the Negro was even there, and you can't be sure, either, gentlemen."

As for Martin's testimony, he said that his friend seemed to dread the thought of being called as a witness as the trouble between Rawlins and Carter escalated. "I told him that if he didn't want to be a part of it, then he should turn his back on it and stay away from it. But I didn't make any threats about Mr. Carter or anyone else. No threats were made at all. None."

Then he addressed the testimony of the preachers. "I hold a minister of the gospel in all sacredness," he said. "I don't want to say that a minister of the gospel told a falsehood, especially on the witness stand and under oath. But it becomes my painful duty to tell you emphatically that Mr. Kemp lied. He said Mr. Carter was stopped from preaching because his license wasn't fixed up right. But I can prove—by the church records in Hahira—that Mr. Carter was turned out of church for cursing and drunkenness. My neck is at stake and it's important that you understand that Mr. Kemp was Mr. Carter's right-hand man during all of his church transactions."

Rawlins directed his next words—and his ire—at the other preacher. "Mr. Tyler said he sent two men, Mr. Touchstone and Mr. Futch to try to buy me and Mr. Carter out. Well, I've never heard of either one of them. If they came to my place, I never saw them. Again, it is my painful duty to tell you that a minister of the gospel got on the stand and testified to a falsehood against a man who is being tried for his neck."

About Gaddy, Rawlins said his former hired hand "lied to me time and time again. He lied to me about needing money to send to his father and I gave him advances on his pay. All that time, Gaddy didn't even know where his father was. Gaddy broke down and cried when I caught him in those lies, cried like a baby and asked my forgiveness. Yes, gentlemen, he told me a whole pack of lies, and he came into this courtroom and lied about what I said to him."

Rawlins said Gaddy's testimony especially hurt "because I treated him with such warmth and kindness. Even after he lied to me, I helped him to get a reduced rate train ticket to get to where his wife and child were. After all that, he proved to be untruthful."

Once on the subject of his own qualities, Rawlins began a spiel that sounded much like a preacher trying to bring sinners back from the edge of the inferno. "How can you believe that a man with the kind of heart I've got—a man who never turned off a single soul, never once in my life turned off a single one...Gentlemen, how can you possibly believe that a man with such a heart as that could lay such a plan—for his own flesh and blood, poor innocent boys—to carry out so atrocious a crime, such a black-hearted crime as has been committed in our part of the country? How can you believe that I would have my boys bloody their hands and stain their hearts for all of eternity? Gentlemen, I say—and I say it in the presence of God and man—that it doesn't sound reasonable, and I say that it didn't happen."

Rawlins looked at his notes and then at the jury. "Now, gentlemen, we come to one of the most painful parts of my story—the testimony of G.A. Fiveash. For truth and veracity, I doubt you can find a man anywhere in Georgia who is more truthful. But G.A. Fiveash swore to a pine-blank lie yesterday evening. That good man, who I thought was the soul of truth and honor, swore to a lie about what I said about Mr. Carter.

"But, if a good man like that G.A. Fiveash gets on the stand and swears to a lie—and the court record will show that he lied—then you must not be surprised that these worthless Negroes were swearing to lies, too. Yes, I come to them at last.

"My boys have been tried and convicted. Under ordinary circumstances, where the sway of the public mind was not already poisoned, they would never have been convicted. But when men such as G. A. Fiveash can be...swayed by public sentiment or whatever it was, it ain't any wonder that a poor, worthless, ignorant, lowdown Negro would also swear against them."

"Mrs. Ella Jones, that poor woman, got up here and testified against me. She has received bread at my hand for her hungry children too many times to mention. Well, she paid me back—every penny—for what I did for her. But I don't blame her. She, too, is ignorant.

"Joe Bentley, the tall, black man, testified I offered him a hundred dollars to kill old man Carter. He is just trying to save his own neck. But do you blame him? I say honestly and positively that I never mentioned any such thing to Joe Bentley or any other Negro or anybody anywhere at any time about exterminating Carter and his whole family.

"Mitch Johnson worked for me and he said I tried to get him to kill the Carters. Now I ask you, gentlemen, does it look reasonable that a man with the kind of sense I have exhibited here would go to this and that and another Negro to kill a whole family? Looks to me like I might as well have come to Valdosta and advertised in the *Valdosta Times* for a man to kill Carter.

"Mitch Johnson is another one I helped. I bought him a suit of clothes. I gave him money in advance and he was always in debt to me. He took off for three weeks because he needed to rest up, and when I asked him to come back, he said he could make more money in public works. He owes me about thirty dollars right now."

Rawlins then asked to see the gun and knife that were entered into evidence. He spent several minutes telling the jury those were not his possessions and offered detailed descriptions of his own guns and knives to back up his assertions.

Then he turned his attention—and his wrath—to Alf Moore.

"They (investigators) reconciled their evidence and then got the Negro to change his story to match the evidence," he said. And he pointed out a list of discrepancies in his testimony and what Rawlins called "the pine-blank truth."

Finally, Rawlins directed an all-out plea at the jury members.

"I have been a man about this matter, gentlemen of the jury, and you know it. My reputation up to the time of this tragedy was as good as any poor man could ask. I had my little home and my family. I had good credit and a good name. I could live out there and go about my business. I was recognized everywhere—including right here in this court. The solicitor general there, he won't look at me now. But as long as I have been in Lowndes County, he has never stricken me from a jury and I have served once or twice every year since I moved here. That solicitor general...Oh, Lord, I hope he has been misled. I know he is doing the wrong thing here, and I hope it does not come from his heart. I do hope he don't get blood on his hands. He has taken steps against me and my boys that are wrong, steps he should not have taken. I say that and challenge him as to whether it is so."

Cooper suddenly interrupted Rawlins and said, "Don't say anything about the prosecuting attorney."

Rawlins: "I didn't know it was wrong to state the facts."

Cooper (wagging a finger at his client): "I don't want you to do that."

Rawlins turned back to the jury and continued, "As far as me hiring anybody, counseling anybody or procuring anybody to molest Carter and his family in any shape, form or fashion...whoever says that is telling a falsehood. If I had been guilty of such an act as commanding my innocent boys to commit such an atrocious crime...Well, gentlemen, I don't believe I would have been able to look honest men like you in the eye ever again.

"The only consolation I have today is that I know I am innocent of this charge, and may God strike me dead on this witness stand if that is a lie."

After Rawlins left the stand, Cooper closed the defense's case. As Rawlins returned to the defense table, moving remarkably better than when he took the stand two hours earlier, Cooper patted him in the shoulder and said he had "done good."

The solicitor recalled two witnesses—Sheriff Passmore and Ed Duggan—to again identify the weapons that were found in Alf Moore's shanty.

Then the state rested.

Before closing arguments began, Cooper requested that the three Rawlins boys be brought to the courtroom to listen to the final words in their father's case. The judge agreed and the sheriff and a couple of deputies went after the prisoners. They returned with just Milton and Leonard.

"Where is Jesse?" Cooper asked.

"He said he would be damned if he would go if he had to wear handcuffs to the courtroom, and I left him in his cell," Passmore said. The sheriff then leaned down and spoke in a low voice so the jurors couldn't hear, "I tried to get him to come, but I wasn't letting him out without chains. He told some of the other prisoners that he was gonna run if he ever got the chance. If he's gonna run, I want him to carry a lot of chain with him."

Cooper nodded to the sheriff and then asked the judge to start closing arguments, that Jesse wouldn't be coming.

Both Thomas and Cooper followed their earlier strategies. Thomas carefully laid out each item of importance and pointed out corroborating evidence and testimony. Cooper again attacked the veracity and accuracy of the testimony of the state's witnesses.

Cooper finally returned to his seat at eight o'clock.

Judge Mitchell, obviously wanting to wrap up the case that evening, charged the jury and sent it into deliberations. There was nothing to do but wait.

As the hours dragged on, the crowd began to drift away, and many of them, convinced that the verdict would be guilty, started the trek back to farms and small communities. Many of the witnesses also headed home.

At 12:45 A.M. on Sunday, word came that a verdict had been reached. Joe Rawlins was asleep on his cot in the courtroom, and when awakened, he showed little interest in the proceedings. The jury foreman handed the written verdict to Thomas and he read, "We, the jury, find the defendant, J.G. Rawlins, guilty of being an accessory to murder."

There was no recommendation for mercy.

Cooper asked for a poll of the jury, and as each man's name was called, he stood and confirmed the verdict.

Judge Mitchell said he would pass sentence at a later date, and Rawlins, looking drowsy and still seemingly unconcerned about the verdict, walked between two deputies to the jail across the street. Few people were there to watch.

But the news traveled quickly. Telephone calls were made to the outlying areas, and voices could be heard in the wee hours of the morning, shouting, "Guilty!" Other voices repeated the one-word message until it reached virtually every corner of Lowndes County.

18

July 31, 1905

FRANK TURNER, LAST OF THE DEFENDANTS IN THE KILLING OF the Carter children, went to trial on Monday morning. Charged as an accessory, he was accused of directing Alf Moore, already convicted as an accessory to murder, to Rawlins for the promise of twenty-five dollars and a new suit of clothes—a debt that was never paid.

Alf Moore was called to the stand once again to tell his story, this time implicating his long-time friend.

The defense did not offer any evidence and after closing arguments, the jury debated about three hours before returning a guilty verdict just after eight o'clock in the evening. Judge Mitchell said he would pass sentence at a later date.

But the day's business was not over. Cooper asked the judge to sentence his clients so the appeals process could begin. The four Rawlins family members were brought immediately from the jail to the courtroom. A capacity audience also was on hand by the time Cooper escorted Angeline Rawlins and the two girls into the courtroom. In a hushed atmosphere, the judge began to speak.

"I have a very sad duty to perform this evening. J.G. Rawlins, will you rise?" After the elder Rawlins stood up, the judge asked, "Do you have anything to say before I pass sentence?"

Joe defiantly said, "My conscience stands as erect as I do. You can no more pluck it than you can pluck the brightness of the sun. The sentence can do nothing but kill. Pass it!"

The judge then read the death sentence, setting September 15 as the day for the hanging. When the judge read the part about being "hung by the neck until you are dead," a smiling Joe Rawlins executed a curtsy and said, "Thank you."

His sons smiled at what they took as bravado on the part of the old man.

Judge Mitchell called Milton Rawlins forward. "It is very sad to have to pass sentence on a young man just growing into manhood, but it should be a warning to all young men who come after you. It is a terrible thing to take a human life, something no man can give and no man should take away. We are told by the scriptures, 'Whosoever sheddeth men's blood, by man shall his blood be shed.' We may conceal crime for a time, but in nearly every case, it will come out and overtake us. It is sad but it is my duty. I have no option or choice."

He then read the death sentence. Milton never uttered a word.

Jesse Rawlins, youngest of all of the defendants, was next. He listened intently as the judge read the sentence, then raised his head slightly and said, "Not guilty."

Leonard was sentenced to the chain gang for life, but the judge added, "It is a serious question whether hanging is not preferable to confinement for life in the penitentiary." The judge said he hoped Leonard would find hope while in prison and that something worthwhile might still come of his life.

When the judge finished speaking, Leonard, too, said, "Not guilty."

With sentencing out of the way, Cooper immediately made a motion for a new trial. A hearing was set for September 9, six days before the scheduled hangings.

As Joe Rawlins left the courtroom, he walked more erectly between the two deputies than at any time during his trial. The boys saw the old man straighten up, and they walked almost proudly as they followed their father from the courtroom.

The following morning, sentence was passed on Alf Moore and Frank Turner, Moore would hang; Turner was given life in prison.

During the two weeks of the trials, Angeline spread the word that the Rawlins farm and brand-new house were for sale. Several prospective buyers approached her immediately after the convictions, but she felt like the best price offered was not enough. So she borrowed money from her father to keep Cooper on the job. Then she summoned her brothers, Gene and Walter, with wagons to begin moving the family's possessions back to Coffee County.

With tears in her eyes, Angeline padlocked her dream house and drove the buggy down the lane and onto the main road toward Valdosta without ever a look back. She and the girls moved into a hotel room temporarily so they could be close to Joe and the boys for at least a few more days.

After two intense weeks of trials and seeing their city overrun with spectators, newspaper reporters and street vendors, most Valdostans were ready to return to a normal pace of life. But that just wasn't to be.

The story of the killings had taken on a life of its own and it would not die. And from all appearances, the *Valdosta Times* didn't want the story to die. If the paper was going to make a successful transition from a twice-a-week publication to a daily, it needed the news and the readership it had built during the sensational trials.

Every time Joe Rawlins or Alf Moore or John Randolph Cooper had something to say, a reporter appeared as if by magic and began scribbling notes. And when one of them seemed not to have anything to say, reporters were tracking down some other angle to the Carter case.

Rumors ran rampant through the county—and beyond. Then the *Times* created a sensation of its own when it reported that, if Joe Rawlins were hanged as planned, he would be a second generation Rawlins to die in such a manner. The paper reported shortly after the trial that Joe's father, James Rawlins, had been hanged years ago in Telfair County.

Three days later, the paper retracted the story, saying it reprinted a story from another newspaper—which remained unnamed—concerning the fate of James Rawlins. However, an affidavit sent by Dr. H. J. Smith of McRae said he had doctored the elder Rawlins until his death in 1880 from old age and paralysis.

This correction was included in a story published August 12, 1905: "The *Times* has no desire to circulate a report that would be prejudicial to anybody, and we take pleasure in correcting the report in regard to Rawlins' father—which was based upon mere rumor."

On the same day, a story in the *Tifton Gazette* reported:

> Members of the ruined Rawlins family, an aged mother (she was forty years old), bowed down in grief, and her two daughters, just touching the threshold of womanhood, passed through Tifton this morning. The mother was returning with her daughters to her childhood home near Ambrose. Her husband and three sons are now in jail in Lowndes County awaiting execution for one of the most atrocious murders to ever blacken the criminal annals of the state.
>
> Mrs. J.G. Rawlins and her daughters, Lola and Leila, were on their way from their former home in Lowndes County to the home of her father, J. J. Jowers, in Coffee County. They were accompanied by her brother, Eugene Jowers.

Mr. Jowers, after some hesitation, talked freely about the case. He said the home the Rawlinses had owned and the land around it made up one of the finest farms in Lowndes County, but it had been sacrificed to pay peace bonds and legal fees. It sold for about five thousand dollars.

Jowers appeared to think there was little hope for the father but expressed hope that the sentences of the boys might be changed to life in prison. Perhaps because of their ages, they might be pardoned some day, he said.

He attributed the boys' connection with the tragedy entirely to the baneful influence of the father, who always exercised an unusually strong control over the boys. He said it was an influence that proved very harmful.

Rawlins, according to Mr. Jowers, appeared very unconcerned over the outcome of the trial and accepted his fate with indifference. Rawlins asked Mr. Jowers to invite his friends to attend the execution.

In Macon, the *Telegraph* reported: "Cooper is strong in his belief that the younger Rawlinses will never hang. He said more than a hundred citizens of the community in which the crimes were committed wanted to sign a petition asking that the death sentences of Milton and Jesse be commuted to life imprisonment."

Three stories in three newspapers on the same day? It was not exactly the peace and quiet the people in Valdosta were seeking.

By late August, Joe Rawlins had told everyone who would listen, "When that Negro, Alf Moore, stands on the gallows, he will tell the truth. When he does, he will admit that he did the killing and he will clear my boys."

The *Times* reported in its August 26 edition:

A very adroit effort was made to get Alf Moore to change his story. Church elder A.V. Sims, after hearing Rawlins talk, decided to see if he could make the Negro tell a different tale about the killings. He first told Alf what an injustice he had done to Rawlins and his sons.

'You have told a story on these people that will cause them to die upon the gallows,' the elder said. 'You have broken up an entire family, swept away their possessions. You are going to drop from the gallows into the bottomless pit of hell unless you confess your lie. Are you going to keep on telling this story, knowing it is not true?'

Moore didn't have to guess where the elder's loyalties lay. But the challenge to his honesty seemed to bother him very little.

"The Negro replied, 'Boss, I like Mr. Rawlins and his boys, and I would not do them any kind of wrong. I know I have got to die and I know that lying on them ain't gonna help my case. I have told the truth—every word of it. And I will die by it. If I told anything other than what I already have told, it would not be the truth and I sho' ain't going into eternity with a lie on my lips. Sometimes I think I'd heap rather do it (lie) than to see them suffer, but I can't do it. I feels for them, but I can't reach them."

The *Times* story said, "The Negro looked as innocent as a child when he said it. The elder Rawlins has said all along that Moore would change his tune before he dies, and he may do it. But there has been nothing in his statement that reveals the slightest variation in what he has said from the beginning.

"Alf is confined in the lower part of the jail and spends most of his nights in prayer. He formerly spent most of his days in a mock trial, but he has quit doing that."

Even the slightest change in any condition of the principals in the case seemed to warrant a story. The *Times* reported: "Sheriff Passmore decided to change Jesse and Leonard from the large cell (where all four Rawlinses had been confined) to cells in another part of the jail. It is said that when Deputy Crosby went to make the transfer, the elder Rawlins protested vehemently as he desired that all of his boys stay with him.

"When he learned that the sheriff's orders were unchangeable, he turned to Leonard and said, 'Leonard, remember now to keep your counsel. Don't talk to anybody and do not trust anybody. Be sure to keep the promise you made to Mr. Cooper.'

"Just what that promise was and why he should keep his mouth shut," the *Times* said, "was left to conjecture."

As the appeal made its way through Lowndes County Superior Court and then to the Georgia Supreme Court, reporters for the *Valdosta Times* continued to stake out the jail and write a story on just about everything that was said. Joe Rawlins, who did almost all of the talking for his family, became very familiar with the reporters. Since Angeline and the girls had returned to Ambrose and visited only every couple of weeks, visits by reporters offered a welcome break from the monotony of his confinement.

During one of those casual visits a little more than two months after the trials, a *Times* reporter found Rawlins lying on his bunk and reading the Bible. On that occasion, the condemned man seemed in a jovial, talkative mood and offered an intimate insight to his state of mind. "How am I doing?" Rawlins repeated the question. "I'm getting along about as well as could be expected, and a whole heap better than I ever thought I would. You see, a man who has led a life like I have finds it pretty hard to be confined in a place like this. Cutting wood, feeding the chickens, looking after the livestock, entertaining the neighbors and quarreling with old man Carter, we had enough to do to keep from getting lonesome. You know, there was hardly a meal eaten at our house that we didn't have company of some sort."

Rawlins stopped and smiled. "Old Carter drove up here in front of the jail yesterday and began hollering to the jailer and the sheriff. He told them if they wanted to lock him up, come on and do it. He did all that to tantalize me and the boys. But he did say we weren't the only ones in it. He yelled out that he didn't want to see the Rawlinses hung unless the whole crowd was gotten. He said I was the captain of the gang but the lieutenants had not been caught.

"Of course he was talking about Tim McDonald, but I tell you Tim McDonald is as innocent of those killings as you are. I know he didn't have a thing to do with it. Old Carter just keeps on trying to stir up trouble."

Asked how he felt about Carter at that point, Rawlins said, "I thought once that I'd forgiven him, but I haven't. It is just one of those things a man can't get out of his mind. I don't believe that Carter wants us hung. This thing has gone further than he expected. I would not be surprised if he wouldn't save our necks if he had the chance. He's in a fearful fix. You see, I believe that the devil gets such an awful hold on a man and, try as he may, he cannot control himself. I believe the devil has got that kind of hold on old Carter. He may change at some point and the spell may be broken, but he's as surely headed to hell as if he was already there."

Did he have any idea this tragedy was going to happen?

"I will answer you indirectly," Rawlins said. "Carter was a nuisance in the community. Many people told me that he ought to be killed. If I had met him on the road and shot him down, nothing would ever have been said. It was the killing of those children that caused such an uproar among the people and caused my friends to turn against me.

"There was bitterness between Carter and myself which had grown with the years. I thought he was going to be killed, but my feeling was such that I did nothing to prevent it. They say that a man who knows a crime is going to be committed and does nothing to try to prevent it is guilty of being an accessory. Of course, I never dreamed that those children were going to be killed.

"But Joe Bentley and Mitch Johnson had asked me so many questions about what old Carter was worth dead that I had a kind of suspicion that they were going to try to kill him for the purpose of robbery.

"Did they do the killing? No. Alf Moore did it. Mitch Johnson put Alf Moore onto it. I thought once that Mitch had a hand in it but the sheriff tells me that Mitch can prove an alibi by Mr. Ivey. That leaves Alf Moore as the sole murderer.

"I'm sure he did not intend to kill the children. The boy came out of the house shooting a rifle. A man could not have committed a crime like that except on the spur of the moment."

Rawlins paused a moment. "I made up my mind twice to kill Carter, once over here in the city hall and the other time in the courthouse. If I had killed him either time, I would have walked away clean as a whistle because he was a nuisance. My friends begged me at the time not to kill him and that is one reason why I did not do it.

"Why am I so bitter toward Carter? Because he is tantalizing and foxy. He has got plenty of fox-sense, but he is the greatest coward you ever saw. You know a fox will slip in the hen house and steal a chicken, and you will never know until it is gone. Carter is that foxy."

Then Rawlins became thoughtful and he said, "The thing I regret most about it all is that the truth may come out too late to save innocent people. You know the stream of falsehood is the hardest thing in the world to cleanse and purify. Did you ever take a basin of pure, fresh water and throw it into a stream of muddy water and watch how quickly it became as muddy as the main stream? The clean water does not cleanse the muddy stream but becomes a part of it.

"Have you noticed a stream of clear water from the mountains—how clear and bold it is? Truth is like clear water, bold and beautiful when allowed to run free. But it is easily muddied and hidden in the stream of falsehood. I wish the truth could penetrate the whole dark chapter of what has happened. If you could hear the whole truth of it, I expect it would make your legs so weak that they would hardly support you."

As the reporter left, Rawlins asked for something to read. "Just anything," he said, "anything at all is good enough for a man in my fix."

When a copy of that story reached Angeline in Ambrose, she made up her mind to pay a visit to her husband—alone. She wanted an honest, private discussion with him. The Georgia Supreme Court would be taking up the case soon and, while she wanted to hold out hope, she had decided on a course of her own that was meant to save her sons from the gallows.

Angeline arrived in Valdosta on October 10 and went directly to the jail. She asked Sheriff Passmore for a private meeting with her husband. She said she might be able to cut through the talk and solve some problems. The sheriff, obviously moved by her earnestness and purpose, allowed her to use his office.

Joe was brought in wearing handcuffs and leg irons. He looked at his wife and said, "What you got under that dress, honey? A pistol? A hammer and chisel for these irons?"

Angeline never smiled and didn't make any show of affection. "Sit down, Joe, and let's talk," she said almost coldly.

"Hey, who put a bee in your bonnet? You look all stirred up."

"I am stirred up, Joe. Sit down and let's talk."

"OK, let's talk."

"I want you to confess your part in this," Angeline said. "Everybody out there thinks you hired Alf Moore to go do this. Papa thinks so, too. And the only way you can save the boys is to confess your part."

Joe was silent, his eyes cast downward.

"Joe, listen to me. You've got to admit it. You should admit it. All of these years, I've listened to you say you hated Carter because he lied about you. You said you could stand anything but a liar. That's what you've said over and over and over. Joe, are you living the biggest lie of all? Is that lie going to put two of our sons on the gallows?"

She paused. Joe was still staring at the floor.

"Look at me, Joe. Damn it, look at me!"

Joe finally looked at her.

"Tell the truth! It's the only way to save the boys!"

She tried to hold back tears of frustration as she waited.

Joe got to his feet and walked to the door. Without looking back, he said, "I'll think about what you said." Then he kicked on the door to get the sheriff to let him out of the office.

Back in his cell, he rolled up in a ball on his bunk facing the wall. He said nothing to Milton. He remained in this curled-up position until sleep overtook him.

Four days later, a crack appeared in Joe Rawlins' armor.

A four-paragraph story buried on an inside page of the October 14 edition of the *Valdosta Daily Times* related a jailhouse conversation from the day before. It said:

"Several gentlemen were in the jail last night talking to J.G. Rawlins when one of them said, 'You know what I believe? I believe you hired Alf Moore to kill old Carter, but you never dreamed the children would be killed. Ain't that so?'

"Rawlins said, 'That's right.'

"The first speaker said, 'If it wasn't that way, you hired him to go and exterminate the family and sent your boys along to help him do it.'

"Rawlins made no reply to the last suggestion, but it evidently had a stirring affect on him."

The newspaper did not identify the visitors who heard the admission, but sent a reporter the next day to ask Rawlins to elaborate. At first, Rawlins declined, but he eventually relented and said the sheriff also should hear what he had to say.

The sheriff called in a couple of witnesses—Tube Swindle, a bailiff, and Orrin Register, a Rawlins friend and neighbor who had been a member of the coroner's jury—to hear the confession.

19

THE *VALDOSTA DAILY TIMES* WAITED UNTIL THE FOLLOWING Tuesday to publish the story about Rawlins' confession from the previous Friday.

Ironically, his attorney, John Randolph Cooper, had left Macon on Monday afternoon to travel to Atlanta to take up the appeal of the case before the Georgia Supreme Court. And on Tuesday morning, while Cooper was making a passionate, tearful plea for a new trial, the people of Valdosta were reading this account of the confession:

"As the sheriff and visitors entered the prison, a jailer was passing a pair of leggings to Rawlins that the prisoner had ordered. Rawlins smiled at the group and said, 'I don't want you gentlemen to think I'm going hunting or fishing. I find leggings more comfortable in this kind of weather.'

"Then he started giving a detailed account of his troubles with Carter over the years. He said he and Carter came from the same county and the fact that he knew much of Carter's past history caused Carter to dislike him and to do all in his power to irritate him.

"Rawlins said, 'Carter hounded me every step I have taken in this county since he came here. He has accused my boys of killing his hogs, me of stealing his mules and attempting an assault upon his wife. He had me in court time and again, prosecuting me or my boys and lying about us. I have gone to my neighbors and begged them to help me. I told them to take up our troubles and see who was wrong. If it was me, I'd sell out and move away, and they would never hear from me again. Mr. Register, you know me, and you know I always have been an honorable neighbor.'

"Mr. Register said, 'I have always said that about you, Mr. Rawlins.'

At that point, the prisoner lost control...and sobbed bitterly.

"Rawlins continued, 'I did everything I could to keep from having trouble with Carter, but he lied about me every chance he got. Do you remember what you wrote to me, Mr. Sheriff, when you sent me one of those papers? You said you were getting tired of mine and Carter's cases. I knew you were tired of them, the public was tired of them and the court officials were tired of them. But what could I do? I had exhausted every means of living in peace with Carter. I went home after we talked that Saturday, and on Monday morning, Joe Bentley came to my house and said he'd found a man who was anxious to put old Carter out of the way.'

"A reporter asked him to name that man. 'Alf Moore, of course,' Rawlins said. 'He did the killing. He never thought about bringing my boys into it until after he was arrested. Then he lied. And Carter would swear away the lives of my boys and the lives of Tim McDonald and his boy just because he doesn't like us. I would gladly lay down my life to lift the stain that has been cast upon Tim McDonald and his family.

"Moore was given positive instructions not to harm any of the Carter children, Rawlins said. In fact, Moore went to Carter's house in the afternoon with the idea of killing the old man while everyone was working in the fields, but he couldn't get Carter to come to the gate. Rawlins says the killing of the children was not in the program and that Moore told Joe Bentley that he killed them when the Carter boy came out of the house firing his rifle. Alf said he fired in self defense.

"Rawlins said, 'Yes, I hired Alf Moore. No, my boys weren't in it. That is the truth and if it isn't, I hope God strikes me dead before I get out of this chair'."

The *Daily Times* added, "This statement appears to be the first determined effort Rawlins has made to shield his sons by taking the blame himself for the Carter murders."

Meanwhile, in Atlanta, John Randolph Cooper, opening what would be a six-hour argument for a new trial for the Rawlinses, seemed to startle the members of the Georgia Supreme Court with his opening statement: "If these defendants are hanged, they will have been mobbed in the name of the law. Yes, I said mobbed in the name of the law. Those men were not given a fair trial in Lowndes County, nor can they get one there.

"The horror of the crime has poisoned the minds of the people there against these three defendants. I know those boys are innocent, and I believe the father is, too. He had nothing against those Carter children. He did not like old man Carter, but he had nothing against the Carter children and certainly didn't want them dead."

At that moment in Valdosta, a reporter was writing still another story about the case. When Alf Moore read about Rawlins' confession, he passed the word that he wanted to talk to a reporter, too. That story said:

"(Moore) walked up to the bars, saw that his visitor was a reporter and said, 'You got me when I wasn't thinking. I'll have to get my head together about what I wanted to say.'

"The reporter asked, 'Do you want to say something about the Carter killing? Do you want to change your statement (made in court)?'

"Moore said, 'Oh, no, I don't want to change a thing, 'cause there ain't nothing to change. A man who is going to die, he ain't got time to be fixing up any tales. I know what Mr. Rawlins has said, that I'll tell the truth just before they hang me. Well, it won't do the old man any good to sit up there and wait to see what I'm going to say. What he ought to do is get himself right. He ought to pray, but…praying ain't gonna do him any good unless he tells the truth. He must throw off his burden and get right with God. Then he can look up and ask for forgiveness and get it.'

"Asked if he had done that, Moore replied, 'I sho'ly have and have not wasted any time about it. I threw off my burden some time ago. There is no blood on my hands and no sin weighs on my shoulders. I have nothing to fear. I like Mr. Rawlins and I like his boys, and I surely would like to help them out of this scrape, but death is too near for me to tell lies for them.'

"Moore then took up the story of the tragedy and told it again just as he had on four occasions on the witness stand. He also voiced a desire to talk to Rawlins and 'refresh his memory on some points.'

"Meanwhile, Moore says he is sticking to his story," the story concluded.

Moore finished his spiel that day; Cooper didn't. The attorney went back on Wednesday morning to finish up one of the more emotional arguments the court ever heard.

"As he approached the end of his appeal," the *Atlanta Constitution* reported, "Cooper burst into tears and begged the court to save those innocent people."

The file Cooper left with the court included more than a thousand pages. His challenge alone accounted for more than one hundred of those pages.

Cooper was not happy when he heard about the confession. He arrived in Valdosta a couple of days later and went directly to the jail. He took Joe Rawlins into a far corner of the cage and away from the boys. Then he turned his wrath on his client.

"Why didn't you tell me you were going to make a confession?" he asked in the tone of a stern schoolteacher dressing down an errant child. "Did you want to make me look like a damned fool in front of the Supreme Court? I was up there trying to convince them that you and your boys are innocent. And what were you doing? Confessing! I told you once before not to spring any surprises on me. What's next, Mr. Rawlins? Are you going to confess for the boys, too?"

Rawlins, whose head had been bowed in shame, suddenly looked the attorney in the eye and said in measured tones, "My boys ain't guilty! Don't you ever say that again. Ever!"

The two men stood eye to eye for several seconds and then Rawlins sat down on a bench. His shoulders sagged and his voice lost its edge as he said, "You can toss me out the window, let me hang. I don't care. But keep working to save my boys. Don't give up on them. They are innocent of this crime. You've gotta save them. You're the only one who can do that for me."

Cooper shook his head in sadness at the sight and sound of the old man's forlorn plea.

"I'm not going to give up," he said firmly.

A rumor swept the city two days after the appeal was argued that a decision had been made. The *Valdosta Daily Times* checked with the clerk of the Supreme Court and denounced that "news" as strictly rumor.

A week dragged by for Rawlins and his boys. Then another. On October 30, Rawlins summoned reporters to his cell and gave another two-hour discourse on his confession and rehashed the feud that led to the murders. He said "plans were laid" by other men on at least two other occasions to kill Carter. One time, Rawlins said, Carter's little girl was in the buggy with him, and on the other occasion, his wife was with him. Both attempts were called off. Rawlins declined to name the men involved.

The *Times* also reported: "Rawlins says he is indifferent about his fate and that he does not care whether the Supreme Court grants him a new trial or not. The only thing that interests him now is the fate of his boys."

By November 3, a Friday, Joe Rawlins was carrying on like a madman, the *Times* reported.

"J. G. Rawlins is said to have put a coat of 'cussing' on court officials and others who were instrumental in bringing him and his sons to this grief," the newspaper said. "Among others, Sheriff Passmore and Deputy Crosby were present. Rawlins talked about the evidence Carter gave at the trial as well as the story told by Alf Moore.

"At one point, Rawlins turned to Crosby and asked if he believed he'd tried to steal Carter's mule. The deputy said he might not have believed it except that another man told him that Rawlins tried to get him to take the mule to Telfair County and sell it. When that man refused, the deputy alleged, Rawlins tied a bundle of fodder to the mule's tail and set it afire. 'See, even that is a damned lie,' Rawlins said. 'It was a bundle of rice straw!'

"At that point, Rawlins branched out into a bitter denunciation of everyone connected with the case on the side of the state. He said his conscience was much whiter than state officials' consciences—'as white as snow is to smut,' he said. Then he shocked everyone by saying that he wished they'd go ahead and hang every member of his family to satisfy the state's craving for blood.

"He was especially severe on Alf Moore during his rambling speech. 'If it wasn't for that nasty nigger, we would be free now,' he said. Rawlins talked on, punctuating what he said with cuss words that fairly sizzled as they rolled off his tongue," the *Times* story concluded.

Afterwards, the sheriff locked Rawlins in a cell by himself "until a change comes over the spirit of his daydreams," the newspaper said.

Rawlins cleaned up his act just long enough to convince the sheriff to let him return to the cell he normally shared with his sons.

"As the day of the decision approached, the mental condition of the elder Rawlins seemed to be in bad shape," the *Daily Times* reported in its November 6 edition.

Rawlins' behavior again became erratic, prompting jail officials and the general public to speculate that he was "going to try the insanity dodge."

"All day Sunday," the *Daily Times* reported, "Rawlins was beating on his cell and yelling at the top of his voice, singing part of the time and crying out to passers-by at other times. A large crowd gathered about the jail to listen to his shouts.

"Finally, his boys said they were afraid for their father to be out in the cage with them. The elder Rawlins said he was afraid of his boys, too, especially Milton who was using a knife a deputy loaned him to eat sugar cane. When Rawlins begged the sheriff to take the knife away from Milton, the boys asked the sheriff to put their father in a separate cell. The sheriff complied with the latter request."

Rawlins was reunited with his sons two days later at the request of the father and with the approval of the sons.

On November 7, the decision of the court was handed down. All of the sentences were upheld by a unanimous vote, except Frank Turner's. The court ruled that, while he was indicted as an accessory to killing W. L. Carter, Carter had not been killed. Since Alf Moore was the main witness against Turner, that decision stayed Moore's execution until court officials in Valdosta decided whether to try Turner on some other charge.

A *Daily Times* reporter beat attorney Cooper to the jail and broke the news to Rawlins and his boys. The reporter filed this report:

"The elder Rawlins took a seat in the cage when the sheriff and the reporter entered. Milton was intently reading a newspaper as though nothing unusual was happening. Jesse and Leonard sat listening.

"When told that the court had affirmed the sentences of Rawlins and his boys and Alf Moore but had overturned Turner's conviction, Rawlins said, 'Well, that's right so far as Frank Turner is concerned. He had absolutely nothing to do with the killings. Alf Moore and Joe Bentley both were careful not to let Frank know about their plans.'

"All the while, Milton went right on reading his newspaper. Jesse showed no emotion whatsoever, but Leonard seemed to be filled with great sympathy for his condemned brothers. The elder Rawlins went right on talking. 'Sheriff, when I told you the other night that I would not care if my whole family, from the baby girl up, was hanged, you said you thought I was either crazy or the meanest man you ever saw. You didn't understand me, sheriff. Thousands of lies have been told in this thing, and maybe it will take a (mass) execution like that to throw light on the truth.'

"Rawlins, with hardly a pause, continued. 'Some mighty good people have had to die the death of martyrs so great truths might come from it. I believe the execution of my whole family might bring about salvation to some who are in desperate need of it.'

"He again asserted that his boys were innocent, and then he continued, 'I have felt sorry a thousand times for what I have done and will regret it as long as I live. I can only say to you and to all, *Watch ye therefore, and pray, lest ye enter into temptation, for at a time when ye know not, the Son of man may come.* I don't feel worthy to let the words of my Savior pass through my lips, but that's the way I feel about it.'

"At that juncture, Milton dropped his paper and looked at the sheriff. 'I believe that you know I didn't have anything to do with that killing, sheriff. I believe Alf Moore has said enough to convince you of that.'

"The sheriff said, 'Alf Moore says every time I talk to him that you were there. He tells the same story now that he has always told. I have tried to shake him, but he won't budge an inch.'

"Milton said, 'A lying scoundrel! I wish that Negro was burned until he told the truth. I'll bet they wouldn't have to touch him but once or twice to get the truth.'

"The elder Rawlins spoke up and said, 'That won't do any good. They'd call that a forced confession.'

"Milton then said, 'Any nigger that would lie like he has lied is sure to go to hell and old Carter will go with him.'

"The old man said, 'Don't talk that way, Milton. I don't think they'll go to hell. They may have found their punishment right here on Earth.'

"Milton said, 'If folks like that don't go to hell, they ought to do away with that place. There are plenty of people mixed up in this thing that ought to have to suffer—if they're not already suffering.'

"Jesse chimed in, 'Oh, hush up, Milton. How do you know who was mixed up in this? You weren't even there.'"

COOPER'S APPEAL OF THE CONVICTIONS WOULD BECOME A model for other attorneys to follow. He offered sixty-one specific challenges to the convictions, including one saying it was unlawful in Georgia to render a verdict on Sunday. The verdict was handed down forty-five minutes after midnight.

Of course, Cooper held the highest hopes on two points— that Moore's confession might be thrown out or that the sheriff's declaration before the jury concerning the pistol in Angeline Rawlins' grip might be reason for a mistrial.

But losing on every point seemed not to deter the young, energetic attorney. He already was certified to argue before the United States Supreme Court, and he announced the highest court in the land would be his next destination.

Exactly who paid Cooper for his services after Joe Rawlins' money ran out was never revealed. One theory held that Cooper absolutely believed that the boys were innocent and took the case without pay. The most common belief was that Squire Jowers pitched in big bucks to try to keep his grandsons off the gallows.

Paid or not, no one could question Cooper's dedication to the Rawlins boys.

Meanwhile, Joe Rawlins was trying a ploy of his own. He'd decided to get Alf Moore face to face and try to break his story — with a few mentions of God, of course.

The two were brought together the evening after the decision of the Georgia Supreme Court was announced. Moore agreed to face Rawlins for the first time since the trials, and Sheriff Passmore escorted him to the cell occupied by Rawlins and his three sons.

Rawlins: "Alf, what made you tell this terrible story on my boys?"

Moore: "'Cause it's the truth, Mr. Rawlins."

Rawlins: "It's a lie, Alf. Do you think you can get to heaven with such a lie in your heart?"

Moore: "I certainly do hope to get to heaven."

Rawlins: "Well, I think you're gonna miss it by about three hundred thousand miles. We are both condemned to hang. I realize I am doomed and I am afraid I am bound for hell. You are certain to go to hell, too, Alf, if you don't repent and tell the truth about this matter."

Rawlins talked for some minutes and quoted a number of passages from the Bible. He finally requested Elder A.V. Sims, who was present, to read one or two directly from the testament. Alf Moore also quoted scriptures and said he was praying for forgiveness for his part in the killings. "I believe the Lord has pardoned my sins already," he said.

After Rawlins asserted again that his boys had nothing to do with the killing, Moore stubbornly challenged the contention and began telling his story again. As he talked, Rawlins frequently interrupted Moore to tell his version of certain events.

More than anything else, perhaps, Moore seemed to resent Rawlins' statement that he gave specific instruction not to harm the children. In a tone much like an attorney might use while questioning a witness, Moore asked, "Mr. Rawlins, didn't you tell me to set fire to the house, to take that gun and kill Mr. Carter and his wife and then kill the oldest boy and girl, and when the little ones ran out, you said to take that knife and cut their throats and throw them back in the fire? Isn't that what you said? Sir?"

Rawlins shook his head side to side and, suppressing a groan, said, "My, my, my."

Moore said sternly: "Don't say, 'My, my, my,' Mr. Rawlins. Answer my question. Ain't that what you told me?"

Rawlins did not answer.

Moore then said, "Let me refresh your memory, Mr. Rawlins." And he continued his account of the case without further interruption. When he finished, attorney Woodard, who had accompanied his client to the cell, asked a few questions of his own.

"Mr. Rawlins, how is it that you can keep murder in your heart day after day, trying to hire Negroes week after week to commit the crime? Can you expect people to try and save you from hanging?"

"No," said Rawlins, "I don't expect it and I won't ask for it. I know I am going to be hung and I reckon I'll go to hell on top of it."

Moore then said he had worked in Coffee County for about three years and wanted to know who told Rawlins that he was at Staunton. Rawlins refused to answer.

The *Daily Times* jumped on this exchange with a question by the reporter. "This (conversation) leads to a rumor that has been in circulation for some time among officials that Rawlins and Alf Moore were in some way connected to the mysterious murder of Hiram Sears in Coffee County several years ago. Rawlins (reportedly) has said a number of times that Moore did the killing. It is also said that Moore has said that Rawlins hired someone to kill Sears. But he did not say who the agent was.

"It is regarded as a little curious that each should lay the killing upon the other, although there is no other evidence that is known to fix the murder on either of them."

20

November 17, 1905

THE *MACON NEWS*, ON INFORMATION PROVIDED BY ATTORNEY John Randolph Cooper, published a story saying "new evidence in the shape of another confession" had been obtained, and "if true, it would free Milton, Jesse and Leonard Rawlins."

This new confession "was secured by J.J. Jowers in Coffee County," the *News* reported, "and implicates another Negro and Tim McDonald, brother-in-law of Sheriff Passmore in Lowndes County."

The *Macon News* also said: "Armed with this confession and many arguments, Mr. Cooper will go before the board of pardons on behalf of the three sons of old man Rawlins. If he fails there, he will go before the United States Supreme Court to fight for the lives of the Rawlins family.

"According to the new evidence...Alf Moore confessed to a Negro named Sam Freeman that old man Rawlins hired him to do the murders. He was assisted in the terrible work by Joe Bentley, a Negro arrested for complicity some time ago and then released, and by Tim McDonald.

"At the time of the alleged confession, Freeman, who was arrested on a minor offense, occupied a cell with Moore. It was then that Moore confessed and said, although satisfied that he will hang, he wanted to tell the truth before he left this world.

"Freeman is now at liberty and lives in Coffee County where Jowers found him and got this evidence," the story concluded.

The next day, the *Valdosta Daily Times* carried a direct rebuttal of the story.

"Alf Moore, who is condemned to die on the gallows for taking part in the murder of the Carter children, was told about the new evidence which lawyer Cooper has found and which will be used before the board of pardons in behalf of Rawlins and his boys.

"It was claimed that Squire Jowers had found a Negro named Sam Freeman who says Alf Moore confessed to him that he killed the Carter children, and Joe Bentley and Tim McDonald aided in the bloody work.

"Moore laughs at the statement and says Freeman is a liar. 'I never talked to Freeman while he was in jail,' Moore said. 'The only thing I know about him is that he stole two or three dollars from one of the other prisoners while we were asleep. If I had him in this cell, I think I would beat that lie back in his mouth.'

"He also was asked about the murder of Hiram Sears in Coffee County and the rumors connecting him with it. 'I can prove by Mr. Wash Lott that I was seven miles from where Mr. Sears was killed when it happened. My name was Alf Moore then just like it is now. Mr. Rawlins tried to get me to kill two or three men, but I never agreed to it. I always thought he had something to do with that Sears murder, but I do not know who did the work for him.'

"It is understood that the lawyers in the Rawlins trial have nearly abandoned the idea of going to the Supreme Court of the United States. But they are circulating petitions to be presented to the pardons board and the governor asking clemency for their clients."

On November 27, Joe Rawlins sent word to Judge Mitchell asking for twenty minutes to make a statement when he was re-sentenced. Rawlins said he wanted to tell the truth and that he would "tell the whole story" if given the opportunity.

"I am the direct guilty white man," the *Daily Times* quoted him as saying. "But there is another white man in this thing, besides the three Negroes."

He did not name the other white man, but he said the Negroes are Alf Moore, Joe Bentley and Henry Rice, the first time the latter name had been mentioned.

Sheriff Passmore went to Rawlins' cell and had a long talk with him after the request was made. Rawlins told the sheriff that he was pretty sure he was bound for hell, but so were the court officials, witnesses and even the jurors. "The whole she-bang is doomed," he said. And he wanted to say so in court.

Rawlins spent much time preparing a statement and, judging from interviews, the *Daily Times* speculated it could be quite lengthy. However, while a condemned person is allowed to make a final statement in the court, the judge has the authority to limit the length of it, the newspaper noted.

On December 1, Joe Rawlins, his sons, and Alf Moore — their appeal denied — were sentenced a second time.

A huge crowd gathered in Valdosta to hear a repeat of the death sentences. It was the largest since the first sentences were passed four months before, the *Daily Times* reported. It was again a mixture of festivities on the streets and somberness in the courtroom.

As the condemned men were led across Ashley Street from the jail, Joe Rawlins drew most of the attention.

"You look pale, Joe," a male voice hollered.

"Ain't much sun coming through that jail window," Joe answered.

One man reached out and stuck several bills in the pocket of Joe's gray coat, and said, "It ain't much, but maybe it'll help."

Joe, his hands cuffed behind him, said in a choked voice, "Thanks, Jimmy. You're a real friend."

In the courtroom, Joe Rawlins looked around. Cooper and Smith, the attorneys were there, but his family was not. He didn't know whether they were absent because they were unaware of the court date or because they didn't want to sit through such a traumatic proceeding again.

Joe Rawlins was first called before the bench. In spite of his earlier plea for twenty minutes to make a statement, he spoke less than five minutes, seemed very subdued and finished with a plea for his sons' lives to be spared. "They are innocent of this crime," he said. "I say that to the people now and I will say it on the gallows when they take me there."

Milton was next. He protested his innocence and then stood silently while the judge read the sentence.

Jesse, who appeared on the verge of tears when he'd entered the courtroom, was more defiant as the judge read the sentence. When Mitchell said, "You have had a fair trial by a jury of your countrymen," Jesse interrupted by saying, "I don't think so." The judge eyed him with a stern expression and said, "The court does." Then he finished reading the sentence.

Alf Moore spoke only a few words in a polite voice, reminding the judge that he had saved Mrs. Carter's life when Jesse started to shoot her and that he had not killed anyone. In any event, he said he had made peace with God and was ready for the hereafter.

Leonard was sentenced to life, and the judge said Leonard should feel thankful that he still had a chance to make something of himself.

All four of the hangings were set for January 6, 1906.

As the prisoners were led away, the crowd on the street again greeted them.

"Don't worry, Joe, we ain't gonna let the boys hang."

Joe smiled a little at that and nodded in the direction of the comment.

As they stepped back in the jail, Joe said to Milton, "Well, it was good to be out of this hellhole for a few minutes anyhow."

Milton agreed.

A week after the sentences were passed, Angeline Rawlins and her daughters came to Valdosta to gather signatures on petitions asking the state board of pardons and the governor for clemency for the boys. For three days, they lived in a hotel room, visited Joe and the boys as much as the sheriff allowed and spent the remainder of their time collecting signatures.

On December 10, Angeline and the girls were at the jail when Sheriff Passmore asked Leonard — in the presence of his mother — to repeat a story he had told the sheriff several days before.

Leonard said on the Tuesday morning before the Carter children were killed, he found his mother crying. When he asked what was the matter, she told him that his father had a Negro hidden out in the fields who was going to kill old man Carter. Leonard quoted his mother as saying such an act would ruin the family.

When Leonard finished telling the story, Mrs. Rawlins acknowledged that the story was true. When the sheriff asked why she had not told the story before, she said her husband threatened to kill her if she breathed a word of it. "He said he might be sent to the chain gang, but he said he would come back and kill me even if he had to wait twenty-five years to do it," she said.

While they were talking, Joe Rawlins took up the story and also said it was true. He said that when he first told his wife about the plot between him and Moore to kill Carter, his wife "took on so" that he was afraid she would tell it in court if he were ever arraigned. That's why he issued the warning that he would kill her if she ever talked about it, Rawlins said.

The *Daily Times* offered this analysis of the family situation: "It is believed by many that the boys would make a statement if they could be taken from under the influence of their father. That's why so many people would prefer that the boys' sentences be suspended until after the old man is hanged.

"If they would acknowledge their guilt and beg for mercy, many people would intervene on their behalf since the public mind is convinced the boys acted under the influence of their father in committing the crime.

"The story about the threat made by Rawlins against his wife shows how the old man has dominated the members of his household so completely."

The paper also noted: "Mrs. Rawlins and the girls were crying much of the time they were at the jail, but they seem to be the only members of the family who are very much stirred up about the sentences. Most of the time, Rawlins and his sons seem completely indifferent about the situation they are in."

While Mrs. Rawlins and the girls were still in town, Warden E.A. Jackson of the Babcock convict camp near Bainbridge came to pick up Leonard Rawlins, touching off another emotional scene. Mrs. Rawlins and her two daughters wept as they said good-bye to Leonard. His father chatted with the warden, telling him Leonard was used to farm work and that his son would work hard if he was treated well. The officer promised good treatment for the boy as long as he obeyed the rules of the penitentiary. Rawlins then lectured his son and extracted a promise from Leonard that he would not try to escape.

The next day, the *Daily Times* quoted Joe Rawlins as saying he didn't want people to sign the petitions his wife and daughters had been carrying around town. He said the petitions indicated that the boys were guilty and he preferred that they were hanged.

His wife engaged Rawlins in a four-hour conversation about the fate of the boys with the sheriff occasionally joining in. Mrs. Rawlins was obviously upset about her husband's remarks and she scolded him for making such statements.

Mrs. Rawlins said, "It is hard enough to deal with this, to try to get people behind the effort for clemency, without you saying, 'Hang us all.' I'm just sick and tired of that kind of talk, Joe."

"Well," said her husband, "I still say hanging is a better way out than spending the rest of your life in prison, and that's especially so for boys this young. Do you know how long they might live to suffer on the chain gang? These boys are strong. They ain't gonna dry up and die in a few years."

He rambled on, but Mrs. Rawlins moved away from him and engaged the boys in conversation, ignoring her husband entirely. And when she left the cell to return to Coffee County, she didn't say good-bye or show any affection. She simply said, "Let's go, girls," and herded them down the hallway and out into the winter sunshine.

The next day, the *Daily Times* carried this story:

> J.G. Rawlins said this morning he wanted to deny a statement attributed to him in the conversation with his wife, the sheriff and others on Monday night and published in Tuesday's paper.
>
> He said a bigger lie was never told. He says Milton and Jesse are innocent and he would rather see them hanged than have to spend the rest of their lives in a penitentiary. To send them to the penitentiary would only give them time to brood over the wrong that has been done to them and would cause a spirit of rebellion to spring up in them.
>
> He said again that death on the gallows was better than a lifetime in prison for an innocent man. And he quoted this scripture: "Fear not that which destroys the body, but rather that which destroys both the body and soul in hell."

Three days later in Atlanta, the Rawlins boys got a boost by someone they'd never met. Judge Andy E. Calhoun, a criminal court judge in Atlanta, appeared before the board of pardons to urge a life sentence instead of hanging for Milton and Jesse Rawlins.

Judge Calhoun said his plea was based solely on his humanitarian instincts and his growing-up years in Coweta County.

"I do not know the Rawlins boys, nor do I know their father. But I understand what kind of boys they are and it would be wrong to deprive them of their lives. I would protest against their sentence if it were the last act of my life.

"I have been a boy and I know the love of a boy for his father. Why, gentlemen, my dear old father could have persuaded me to commit any crime and I would have gladly obeyed his command without ever stopping to count the cost or to think whether it was right or wrong.

"In my home county of Coweta, there are people today whom I do not like simply because they were not liked by my father. I know nothing of them one way or another. The influence of my father and my profound respect for his judgment about all matters simply made me dislike his enemies, though I had no knowledge of them.

"The Rawlins boys were unfortunate in having for a father a bloodthirsty, vicious old man. They were not reared properly, and when their father planned the atrocious murder of the innocent little Carter children, the boys executed the deed without hesitating to count the cost.

"I think the boys ought to be punished. Their sentences should be commuted to life imprisonment, and their old father, who planned the heinous crime, should he hanged half a dozen times if necessary.

"I understand these boys, and I beg you to spare their lives."

Outside the hearing room, one of several reporters gathered in the hallway asked Judge Calhoun why he was appearing before the board of pardons if he did not know the Rawlins boys and had no connection to their case.

The judge pointed a finger at the reporter and said, "You don't get it, do you? You just don't get it. These boys are guilty of blind obedience. Nothing else. Certainly not murder."

He paused a moment and then added, "I said they are guilty only of blind obedience. Do you get it now?"

Another prominent resident of South Georgia sent a written plea to the board of pardons. J.A. Henderson of Ocilla, president of the Ocilla & Valdosta Railroad, also asked for commutation of the sentences.

Henderson said the fate of the boys became a matter of concern at his church. He, too, cited the ages of the boys and the "overbearing influence of their father" as reasons to keep them off the gallows.

He made no appeal for mercy on behalf of Joe Rawlins or Alf Moore.

Since attorney Cooper had publicly announced his plans to take the appeal to the U.S. Supreme Court a second time, the letter and other pleas and petitions were filed away to wait until all litigation at all levels was exhausted. The board of pardons, after all, was meant to be a station of final appeal.

21

Spring 1906

ATTORNEY COOPER MADE GOOD ON HIS PROMISE TO TAKE THE case to the highest court in the land. He filed an appeal on grounds similar to those the Georgia Supreme Court turned down.

But, for all of Cooper's endeavors, his clients' morale and confidence began to crumble, and they were showing anything but a unified front.

Sheriff Passmore observed that with the start of the new year — 1906 — Joe Rawlins became one of the most troublesome inmates ever lodged in the Lowndes County Jail. In a matter of days, he became an outcast even in a cellblock of outcasts.

First, he alienated his sons with constant assertions that it was better to hang than to spend a lifetime in prison. When Milton told his father that he was tired of hearing it, the elder Rawlins began quoting scriptures in support of his contentions. Finally, Milton, whose temper was every bit as explosive as his father's, ripped a metal slat from a bunk and shouted to the sheriff that he was going to "kill my old man if you don't take me out of this cell."

As the sheriff approached the cell, Milton shouted at his father, "You've always treated your children like puppies and your wife like a dog. There is not a place on my back or on my mother's back that is not scarred by licks you gave us. And now you have brought this on us. You are to blame for the whole thing. You acted like a nigger and put yourself at the level of that black rascal, and this is the result."

As the sheriff ordered Milton to put down the slat, his father said, "Well, well, why not tell the whole business, Milton? Let's tell the whole truth. It ain't been half-told yet. Let's tell it all and let the chips fall where they may. I've been taking all of the blame. Let's let the facts be known."

Milton started to offer a rejoinder, but Jesse cut him short. Although the youngest of the three boys, he usually had the cooler head. He cut in with, "Hush up, Milton. Too much has been said about this already."

Milton dropped the slat, ending the confrontation with his father, but he still insisted on moving out of that cell. The sheriff took Milton to a new part of the jail. Jesse said he wanted to move, too. With Leonard already sent to the convict camp, the old man was without the company of any of his boys for the first time in months.

As soon as the boys reached the new cell, Jesse told the sheriff he would like to see Alf Moore. He told the sheriff that Moore wouldn't recognize him if he walked into that section of the jail. The sheriff, obviously needing some nonviolent entertainment, agreed to let Jesse disguise himself as best he could with an old hat lying on one of the benches in the cage, and followed him to the lower floor of the jail where Moore was being held.

When Jesse spoke to Moore, the condemned man walked to the bars and said in a kindly voice, "Hello, son, how are you getting along?"

Jesse said, "Do you know about me?"

Moore smiled and said, "Sure, I know you. I see'd you at Mr. Carter's house. You're Jesse. I know you."

As an amused Sheriff Passmore motioned Jesse out of the area, Moore called out, "There ain't no use to deny it, son. I saw you carrying shucks to the house. You almost was shot by Mr. Carter. Remember Milton hollering, 'Is you hit? Is you hit?'"

Moore, obviously pleased with himself, laughed heartily as the sheriff led Jesse back to his cell.

With the boys gone, Joe Rawlins slipped into a state of depression unlike anything the sheriff had ever seen. Sometimes the prisoner wandered aimlessly about the cell. At other times, he'd sit on his bunk and read his Bible out loud in the booming voice of an old-time preacher. In fact, he shouted scriptures at times that could be heard on the street. And he repeatedly asked anyone who would listen if he had "committed the unpardonable sin."

He wrote a letter to the *Daily Times* and expounded on the unpardonable sin theory. Seeing his letter in print seemed to calm the elder Rawlins — for a couple of days.

When word came on January 23 that the hangings would be delayed at least until April, Rawlins returned to his earlier boisterous and disrupting ways.

First, he shouted epithets from his cell that "polluted the ears of women and children passing the jail," the *Daily Times* reported.

Next, he picked an argument with one of his new cellmates, a pickpocket. The new inmate told the sheriff that if Rawlins didn't quit his complaining and incessantly quoting scriptures, he was going to save the state the trouble of a hanging.

When the sheriff started to dress down Rawlins for bothering the other prisoners and cursing loud enough to be heard on the streets, Rawlins threw a syrup bottle at the sheriff. Passmore told Crosby that, had he not dodged, the missile might very well have inflicted serious injury.

As the sheriff searched for a solution, Rawlins ripped loose a pipe in the brand-new plumbing in his cell and used it to beat on the bars as water flooded his cell and leaked into other cells on the lower floor. As soon as the water was turned off, Passmore and two jailers entered the cell and took the piece of pipe from Rawlins. The sheriff warned the prisoner that his conduct would not be tolerated.

With the water cut off, Rawlins refused to take a bath using a basin of water provided and began running about his cell stark naked. Women visitors were kept from the jail for two days while the sheriff sought a solution.

Finally, Passmore, normally a congenial man, put Rawlins in chains and locked him away in a cell in the darkest corner of the jail. He then hung blankets around the cell to bring almost complete darkness.

"My lawyer is going to sue you for this," Rawlins shouted from behind the wall of blankets.

Passmore shouted back, "Your lawyer has had enough of you, too. He might want to buy me a steak dinner."

Twenty-four hours later, Rawlins called to the sheriff, promising to mend his ways. The sheriff took down the blankets as a probationary measure and told Rawlins he could return to his regular cell in two days if he "acted right."

By mid-February, Rawlins was back in a letter-writing mood, this time telling Cooper to abandon the appeals process because he wanted to "go ahead and hang and get it over with."

Cooper wasn't listening. He'd been assigned a date—April 2—for arguing the case before the United States Supreme Court. Preparations for that hearing were uppermost in Cooper's mind. He'd never wanted to win a case any more than this one.

As Cooper studied the law, Rawlins was shouting a sermon out the window of the Lowndes County Jail. He told an audience gathered on the street outside, "I tell you there is no hope for a man who falls from grace. If the Bible is true, there are going to be mighty few people saved from damnation. The liars, the thieves, the back-biters, those who are puffed up with pride—as well as the murderers—are going to be cast into eternal darkness. If many shall knock and few shall enter, what hope is there for a man who has gone as deep into sin as I have?"

A voice from the street shouted, "Do you believe you were ever in grace?"

Rawlins shouted back, "I know I was. When I came to this county eight years ago, I was a God-fearing, sin-hating man and my neighbors would tell you so."

Another voice shouted, "You ain't never been in grace, Rawlins. You always was a sinner!"

Rawlins eyebrows raised and he shouted back, "Is that you, Carter. Hey, somebody tell me, is old man Carter out there?"

He didn't get an answer.

Slowly, he sank down on his cot and said, "I am lost in sin. I will sink into a sea of fire and brimstone."

On the last day of February, word came that the governor had delayed the hangings until after the case was heard by the U.S. Supreme Court. Joe Rawlins offered still a different reaction to the delay. He acted like he didn't care one way or the other. But Sheriff Passmore soon found out that Rawlins was just playing 'possum.

An attempted escape by two pickpockets who shared a cell with Joe Rawlins was thwarted in late March. The prisoners, using hacksaw blades—which they said they lifted from a plumber's toolbox while the pipes were being repaired—cut through ten bolts before their plan was discovered.

Sheriff Passmore believed that Joe Rawlins was involved in the escape attempt but wasn't sure he could prove it. Besides, he had no desire to make an attempted escape charge against Rawlins. That could mean a delay in the hanging, and the sheriff, like almost everyone else who'd had anything to do with Joe Rawlins, didn't want any more delays.

Three days after the escape plot was uncovered, attorney Cooper made an hour-long argument before the Supreme Court in Washington. The panel of judges was not impressed with the points raised by Cooper. At the end of an hour's presentation, the court announced it found no merit to

Cooper's argument and did not care to hear anything else, not even from the state's lawyers.

Cooper, unfazed at being summarily dismissed by the high court, promptly mounted two new appeals — an insanity plea for Joe Rawlins and a motion for clemency for the boys. Cooper also was preparing an appeal to the board of pardons based on "the complete control" the elder Rawlins had over his sons. An earlier appeal had been successful for a North Georgia boy whose father had gotten the son intoxicated before sending him out to commit a robbery.

On April 10th, Joe Rawlins talked at length with his sons for the first time in months. The *Daily Times* reported that the elder Rawlins "was in better humor than he has been in a long time." Rawlins implored his sons to "be brave, that innocent men have died upon the gallows before." Milton had little to say during the hour-long visit.

On the same day the *Daily Times* informed its readers about a massive earthquake in San Francisco, another jailhouse story said Rawlins and his sons would surely get still another reprieve while the results of the appeal was working its way from Washington, D.C., to Valdosta.

When Joe Rawlins heard about the delay, he said, "Well, Passmore has been elected again, so let's get on with the hangings. I sho' would rather have the devil to contend with than this sheriff."

Meanwhile, Leonard Rawlins was brought back to Valdosta from the convict camp to stay until all appeals were exhausted. His son's presence pleased Rawlins, and for several days, an unusual peacefulness settled over the jail.

Sheriff Passmore was overheard saying to Crosby, "If that kid will keep the old man quiet, I guarantee he ain't going back to the convict camp."

On May 2, Governor Terrell announced he probably would sign another reprieve, delaying the hangings until at least June 8.

The governor told Cooper he was granting his last reprieve in the case and would personally work to cut any red tape meant to delay the executions again.

On May 10, Henderson, the railroad president from Ocilla, filed a petition signed by seventy-five Irwin County residents asking the board of pardons to commute the boys' sentences. The board agreed to take up the matter, but a date was not set.

While Cooper was working the legal system, Joe Rawlins fired off another letter to the attorney, telling him to stop pushing the petitions, saying that the petitions were a sign of guilt and that he didn't want anything to imply his sons were guilty of murder. In fact, Rawlins contended, the petitions were part of a conspiracy.

"The best men in this town are against those petitions," Rawlins wrote, "but those who have done the dirty work are greatly elated because they know the petitions will keep what they have done concealed."

Cooper ignored Rawlins and filed still another appeal with Lowndes County Superior Court, using Joe Rawlins' confession made nine months earlier as grounds for a new trial for the boys.

Judge Mitchell held a short hearing and turned down the appeal.

Cooper's expertise in the courtroom irritated Lowndes County officials, especially the sheriff. Without meaning to pass any compliments, Passmore stated in a letter to the editor of the *Macon News*, "Mr. Cooper's tactics (are) wily and his 'sharp' maneuvers are causing a delay in carrying out the law" in the Rawlins case.

While Cooper waited hopefully to argue the case a second time in Atlanta, Sheriff Passmore decided to begin building a double scaffold. Since virtually all of the nation's executions were held in "private," the most likely place for the gallows to be erected was in the lower part of the jail where black prisoners were detained.

As lumber was being hauled into the "courtyard" of the county jail, news reached Valdosta that attorney Cooper was involved in a train wreck in Macon. The report said he'd sustained "only painful bruises."

Joe Rawlins laughed uproariously and said, "I see my wish came true. Didn't you know I was wishing that a train would run off the track and kill Cooper?"

Indeed, Rawlins had been reading a newspaper account of a train wreck several days before and had wished just such a fate for Cooper.

"You're a sick man," Jailer John Hester told Rawlins.

"Yeah," Rawlins answered, "and in a few days I'm going to be a dead, sick man. The jig is up. Me and Alf will hang next Friday, and when Alf gets on the gallows he's going to squeal like a stuck pig and he will clear my boys."

Rawlins surely thought his time had come when the Georgia Supreme Court turned down the second appeal on July 27. He fired off a letter to Governor Terrell, pleading for the sentence to be carried out on August 3 as planned.

But Cooper wasn't ready to throw in the towel.

"There will be no hangings on August 3," he told The Macon Telegraph. "It will be at least thirty days before the sentence can be carried out. Ten days are required for the remittur (the high court's written decision) to go down (to the lower courts). Then the judge is obliged to give them twenty days (before being hanged). Before thirty days have passed, I will have another action by which to save them."

Again, he was right.

The Associated Press reported, "John R. Cooper, attorney for the Rawlinses, took out a habeas corpus proceeding before Federal Judge Emory Speer in Macon on Saturday, but the judge declined to grant the writ. However, Judge Speer did certify Cooper's appeal to the United States Supreme Court. Given that development, the executions cannot be carried out before sometime in October."

Facing a firestorm of criticism, Judge Speer explained that the matter of whether the jury list was legal appeared to be a constitutional matter and should be taken up by the United States Supreme Court.

Ironically, the decision was based on the fact that Rawlins had been an ordained minister and ministers were systematically excluded from the Lowndes County jury list. Therefore, Cooper contended, Rawlins had not been tried before "a jury of his peers," a right guaranteed by the U.S. Constitution.

When legal scholars heard Judge Speer's reason for sending the case to the U. S. Supreme Court, the mere possibility that this upstart lawyer might get a favorable ruling sent tremors through the judicial system.

The Associated Press said, "It is the first time in the history of this state that the system of jury boxes has been attacked. If this motion is sustained, it could affect the entire system of selecting jurors in this state as well as just about every state in the union. A special session of the legislature would have to be called to remedy the state's system for selecting jurors."

On July 28, the gallows in the jail at Valley and Ashley streets was completed. The trapdoor that had been installed was big enough to carry out a double hanging. One of the main supports for the structure was so close to Alf Moore's cell that he could reach out and touch it.

22

EXACTLY ONE YEAR AFTER JOE RAWLINS WAS CONVICTED, HE was still at least three months away from hanging. Although the latest respite concerned only the elder Rawlins, the state was not going to put Alf Moore, its star witness, on the gallows ahead of Rawlins. His testimony would be crucial if a new trial were ordered. And virtually no one believed that the boys would be hanged before their father. In fact, sentiment was building for the boys' death sentences to be commuted to life in prison.

Cooper's delaying tactics came under heavy fire from newspapers. His methods were called "devious," "lacking substance," and "meant only to enhance his reputation."

On August 2, however, Governor Terrell again issued a stay for the elder Rawlins and Alf Moore until October 5. Reminded by the press of his earlier statement about no more appeals, he said he had "no choice under the circumstances."

When this news reached Valdosta, a persistent rumor said certain parties were ready to take the law into their hands and carry out the execution in the form of a lynching. When Cooper heard about it, he rushed to Atlanta and implored the governor to call out the militia if necessary to ensure the safety of his clients. The governor called Lowndes County officials and he was assured that no lynching was going to take place.

Solicitor Thomas also heard the rumors and talked to the crowd which gathered outside the jail every day to discuss the case and listen to Joe Rawlins. Thomas encouraged those present to "let the law take its course."

Meanwhile, the *Daily Times* uncovered an inconsistency in Joe Rawlins' stand on the hangings. Rawlins sent a telegram to Governor Terrell on August 2, saying, "Please let me hang tomorrow." The newspaper revealed the prisoner had sent a telegram a few days earlier to Cooper, saying, "For heaven's sake, don't let them hang me on Friday."

The newspaper asked the questions on everyone's lips: "Does Rawlins want to be hanged or does he want to remain on top of the earth to enjoy the sensation which he creates from his prison cell? Is his hatred of attorney Cooper real or is it feigned?"

On August 6, Cooper came under fire once again when the Associated Press reported there was "a very strong possibility that the United State Supreme Court will censure attorney Cooper for the latest trick he has turned in the Rawlins case."

On the same day of the AP story, the *Atlanta Morning News* called on the Georgia Bar Association to police its ranks. "The time has come," an editorial said, "for the Georgia Bar Association to take some action to prevent frivolous appeals and technical delays in criminal court trials. This is especially important in cases of criminal assault on white women and in cold-blooded murder cases. John R. Cooper is a shrewd attorney, gifted in the art of conjuring up special pleas to save the necks of his clients."

Cooper obviously intended to use every ploy he could, even though he was working for a client who constantly criticized him and interfered with his efforts. While the press continued to verbally batter Cooper, Rawlins leveled still another barrage at his lawyer.

The *Daily Times* reported, "Rawlins said he had tried every conceivable way to get Cooper off the case and had failed. 'Don't you see that he just aggravates the public?' Rawlins asked. 'He's got people clamoring for our blood. Didn't you see them editorials in that Atlanta paper where they were trying to incite a lynching?'"

When Rawlins offered that comment, his son made a startling revelation: Joe Rawlins had once led a lynch mob.

When a mob tried to lynch the two murderers of Henry Vickers several years before, the effort had been foiled by lawmen. "Foiling that mob and hanging the murderers by law had a good effect," a *Daily Times* reporter said. "That might be why you haven't been lynched."

At that point, Jesse Rawlins said, "The old man led that mob."

Joe Rawlins said, "Well, I was pushed into it. They came to my house after I had gone to bed and told me about it, and I joined them. They didn't have a leader, so I was decided to be the general in charge. But that was the worst experience I ever had, and it cured me forever of wanting to join a mob again."

Rawlins railed against each delay.

When Cooper went before the board of pardons on behalf of Milton and Jesse, he asked a reporter, "Don't you see through the whole scheme? Can't you see a conspiracy to force these boys to go before the pardons board so it will let the nigger do the same thing? They (court officials) don't want the truth to come out. They want to keep it hidden. If Alf Moore confesses on the gallows, it shows that innocent boys were sentenced to hang. They would rather hang my boys than to be proven wrong. If Alf Moore's sentence is commuted, he goes free in a couple of years and the truth will never come out. Alf Moore must be put on the gallows for the truth to come out. Don't you see that?"

When the reporter seemed hesitant to agree with him, Rawlins picked up his Bible and said, "Do you read this? What happened to David, a man after God's own heart, when he committed that sin? Why did he put Uriah in front of the army if it was not to get rid of the evidence of his own sin? My God, how I wish that we had men today who, like that priest who faced David, would point his finger and say, 'Thou art the man.'"

On September 15, almost a year after his conviction was overturned by the U.S. Supreme Court, Frank Turner was finally allowed to sign a $500 bond and was released. The *Daily Times* reported:

> The Negro was kept in jail for the purpose of trying to get up more evidence against him, but as this was not forthcoming, he was released. Turner is said to have gone from here to Hahira, met an old friend, George Robinson, and asked how the feeling was about him. Robinson replied, 'Everybody is against you. They will kill you if you stay around, and I am mad enough to help them.' Others... advised him to leave, and he has not been seen since.

On September 21, Jesse and Milton Rawlins issued an appeal to the public to try to influence the governor to set their execution date twenty to thirty days after Alf Moore's execution in order to get him to tell the truth. "We are not trying to get Alf Moore hung," the statement said, "but this is the only way we can see to prove our innocence. Almost all murderers confess on the gallows, and we think Alf will."

Moore immediately replied in a letter to the *Daily Times*: "I haven't killed anyone to be hanged for, but to satisfy Mr. Rawlins and to let him see that I will not change my statement, I am willing to be hanged first."

Moore also wrote: "I think, however, he (Rawlins) wants me killed first because he didn't get a chance to carry out his plan. I am convinced that he intended to kill me after everything was over. But he was in custody and never got the chance. I think the spirit is still there for him to kill me or see that someone else does it for him."

On October 1, the day before Jesse and Milton were scheduled to hang, the AP reported, "A tearful plea before the governor by Mrs. Rawlins has secured an additional respite of thirty days for each of the boys. Her father, Squire Jowers, and attorney Cooper presented the governor with a petition signed by 800 people urging the action. Mrs. Rawlins assured the governor she would produce convincing evidence for a new trial when the hearing before the board of pardons comes up on October 13."

When Cooper cited Joe Rawlins' "complete control over his sons" as reason for the respite, Rawlins became publicly critical of his wife for the first time.

"My wife has gone back on me," he said. "She was there and she ought to have stood up the moment Cooper said that if anybody sent them to help Moore, it was me. I cannot understand why she would let that statement stand. She knows it is not true. She knows I did not send those boys with Alf Moore. I was in town. If anybody sent those boys . . ." He stopped short, but the implication was that if anybody sent the boys, it had to be his wife.

On October 26, the board of pardons said it would make no decision until Joe Rawlins' case before the nation's highest court was settled.

On October 30, three days before the boys were scheduled to hang, the governor signed another reprieve for Alf Moore and the Rawlins boys. Moore would hang on November 30, he said, and the boys one week later.

In Washington the following day, Cooper took his appeal for Joe Rawlins before the U. S. Supreme Court a second time. The high court turned down the appeal one week later.

In Valdosta, Rawlins told the sheriff, "I wanted to end this, but people didn't believe me. Maybe they will believe me when they see how quick and eager I will go to the gallows."

Then he began a sermon, quoting the eighteenth chapter of Revelations, reading some passages a second time for emphasis. When a *Daily Times* reporter and the sheriff left his cell, Rawlins was loudly singing, "Cheer up, brother, cheer up; these trials will soon be o'er." He sang three verses and then began whistling the tune, the shrill notes loud enough to be heard a block away.

On November 12, Judge Mitchell set the elder Rawlins' hanging for the fifth time—for December 3. The judge said before a packed courtroom that he wanted to give Rawlins the full twenty days usually accorded a condemned person between sentencing and hanging, and since the twentieth day fell on Sunday, December 2, he had decided to set the hanging on Monday.

Cooper went back to court, appealing to Judge Speer to intervene once again by saying that if certain records had accompanied the previous appeal to the Supreme Court, a new trial might have been granted. The judge said he would entertain no more "frivolous applications," and if Cooper continued to abuse court proceedings, he might have to "take action" against the lawyer.

Still, the delays were not over. The Methodist Conference of South Georgia would be in session in Valdosta on the day set for the execution, and the meeting place was just a block from the jail. Local officials told the governor a hanging should not be carried out in such close proximity to a religious conference.

On November 21, the board of pardons in Atlanta announced that it would wait until after Joe Rawlins was hanged to rule on commutation of the boys' sentences.

In Macon on the same day, Cooper announced that he would let Rawlins have his wish and hang. He said he would concentrate on saving the boys from the gallows.

On November 23, Governor Terrell, who'd said emphatically six months before that he would issue no more reprieves, granted one more. He moved the execution of both Joe Rawlins and Alf Moore to December 4. Sheriff Passmore said the two men would hang side by side—same scaffold, same trap door, same trigger.

On November 26, five days after he said he was washing his hands of Joe Rawlins' case, attorney Cooper surprised everyone by making another effort to save his client. He made a motion before Judge Mitchell in Valdosta, asking that the sentence be set aside because records of the trial did not show that the Rawlinses were present at their trials or sentencing. The judge ruled that the appeal appeared to be trivial and meant only to delay the execution.

Two days later, an undaunted Cooper appeared before the Georgia Supreme Court with the same motion, asking the high court to set aside the verdicts against Joe Rawlins and his sons.

Later that same day, the high court said it would not consider that motion.

Had Cooper finally run out of legal options?

23

November 30, 1906

JOE RAWLINS, FINALLY REALIZING TIME MIGHT BE RUNNING OUT for him, sent a message that caused all sorts of speculation. He told a jailer he wanted to confer with Rev. M. A. Morgan as soon as possible. Was he going to reveal new information? Was he going to change his mind about further appeals? What was behind Rawlins' sudden desire to see the preacher?

The minister, a regular visitor to the jailhouse, thought Rawlins needed spiritual help and hurried to his cell. But when Morgan arrived, the condemned man was not in a repentant mood. In fact, he was far from it.

"I just want to tell you," he said in his usually loud voice, "that I think the preachers have done wrong in getting Alf Moore's sentence postponed. The preachers are going to have blood on their hands. If they had let Moore hang on Friday, he would have told the truth about all this and my boys would have been set free. I blame the preachers for the delay of Alf's hanging, and it done me and my boys a great injustice. I want you to tell all of them preachers I said so."

Morgan advised Rawlins that the devil was working to keep him mad at people. If Rawlins felt the need for spiritual comfort, the preacher said he would be happy to provide it. But he would not argue matters concerning his case, nor would he furnish others for Rawlins to argue with. And he left the jail.

Later in the day, Rawlins' close friend Tim McDonald came to Joe's cell. After the Rawlins boys greeted McDonald and went back to reading or talking to other prisoners, Joe stood close to the bars and motioned his friend away from the others.

"You gonna kill old Carter for me, ain't you, Tim?"

McDonald looked surprised. "You ain't heard, Joe?"

"Heard what?"

"Well, Carter moved away as soon as he got his crops in last month. He's long gone. Moved out."

"I still want you to kill him."

McDonald stood looking intently at Joe for a moment and then he shook his head. "Joe, it's over. Ain't no more fighting out there, no more shooting—it's peaceful like it used to be. Like it was before you and Carter got into it."

Rawlins stared at McDonald in disbelief. "Carter is gone? Where?"

"Berrien County, I heard."

"And you're just gonna let him ride away after all the grief he brought us?"

McDonald shook his head again, reached through the bars, patted Rawlins on the arm and said, "See you, Joe." And he left.

Rawlins held onto the bars for a long time and stared after his friend.

Finally, he said aloud, "Don't seem to be no justice at all in the world sometimes."

"Yeah, Pa, you're right," said Milton, even though he didn't know what the two men had been talking about.

On November 30, Rawlins said he didn't want the board of pardons or the governor to take any action on the case unless he and the boys were given a new trial.

But even as he issued that statement, Cooper was on his way to Atlanta to ask for a plea for mercy before the board of pardons. He also filed an appeal with the governor.

On December 3, the day before the scheduled hangings, two telegrams arrived at Cooper's office and copies were sent to Sheriff Passmore. One came from the governor, saying he would grant no more respites. The other informed Cooper and his clients that the next meeting of the board of pardons would be held on Thursday, two days after Rawlins and Moore were to be hanged.

Joe Rawlins grew violent on his last day, the *Daily Times* reported. "His passion has driven him to use strong language, much as a Negro preacher does when the spirit moves him. He has been visited by a number of ministers and friends, while crowds have stood about the jail all day long.

"Rawlins' denunciation of the courts, the lawyers, the preachers, the newspapers and the government itself could be heard two blocks away. Rawlins said he had been railroaded to the gallows by his own attorneys."

Rawlins quoted the Bible about spirits that come back to haunt. "When I am dead and gone, I want my spirit to come back and haunt court officials to the end of their days," he told the *Macon Telegraph*.

About newspapers, he said, "Nine hundred and ninety-nine in every one thousand newspaper editors will go to hell because they are too cowardly to fight against public sentiment."

Finally, Rawlins launched into a lengthy rehashing of the trial. And when he finished a scorching attack on the courts and lawyers, he added, "I will go to hell, but I will spend my time heaping coal on the fire for judges and lawyers."

Later in the day, Rawlins settled down when his wife and daughters appeared. He chatted with them just like it was a normal day in his life, not mentioning the event planned for the next day. He also took time with a lawyer to make sure his insurance policies, worth about four thousand dollars, would be paid to his wife.

He hugged his whimpering daughters a couple of times, but never showed any affection toward his wife.

When Alf Moore was told late in the afternoon that the governor would not give him a respite, he told reporters that he felt like he had not been treated right.

"I didn't kill anyone and I told the truth," he said, "just like they said I ought to tell it. I think I am being hung just to satisfy Mr. Rawlins. He don't want to make this journey alone... but I think we are heading in different directions. I'm right with God. I'm going to heaven."

He turned to a preacher who had been praying with him throughout the day and said, "You'll meet me there, won't you, brother?"

The preacher nodded vigorously, raised a hand upward and began to pray aloud.

Joe Rawlins remained up late that last night, talking to people who crowded about the jail to listen to him and ask questions. When ten o'clock came, the death watch guard told him he had to leave the cage and go into his cell. Rawlins begged for more time outside the cell, but the guard would not permit it.

"I wish I had asked the sheriff if I could stay up all night with these people," he said. "I feel like talking."

From his cell, he continued a loud conversation with people on the street well into the night. Other prisoners did not complain. On other nights, they might have, but Joe Rawlins would have no other nights to talk.

Joe was up early on his last morning. He resumed his conversations with the crowd outside the jail. More than a thousand people had gathered, and they were attentive to every word the condemned man uttered.

Then he looked at a *Daily Times* reporter who had arrived early and said, "You can come to the hanging, too."

"Have you slept any?" the reporter asked.

"Not much," Rawlins answered. "I'm like a child going on a long journey. The anticipation of it kept me awake. You know young children don't sleep much when they're going on a long journey."

Slim Griffin, a holiness minister of street-preaching fame, yelled from outside the jail, "This is Slim Griffin. I'm going to wire the governor right now and tell him the followers of Jesus Christ want this sentence commuted."

Rawlins hollered back, "Don't you reckon the governor will wire back to find out who Jesus Christ is?"

Laughter erupted on the street. At nine o'clock, local ministers from several denominations arrived and spent almost an hour with Rawlins. They implored the condemned man to surrender his life to the Lord. Rawlins did not mention his earlier contentions that nothing could keep him from going to hell. In fact, Rawlins seemed quite indifferent to pleas by the preachers for repentance.

At ten o'clock, Angeline and the two girls, Lola and Leila, were escorted into the cage and several reporters also were admitted. A suit of black clothes was brought for Rawlins to wear to the gallows. As his father dressed, Leonard began to sob uncontrollably. His sisters joined in. Angeline bit her lip but refused to shed any tears in front of the crowd of men.

Rawlins walked to his cell and pulled a bottle from under his cot. He said it wasn't a drug but it would "fortify" him and steady his nerves. Finally, he became impatient with the sheriff.

"I wish he'd come on," Rawlins said. "I'm tired of waiting."

He looked at his boys sitting in a nearby cell and said to no one in particular, "I don't think they'll hang my boys. They're going to send them off to a penitentiary and make devils out of them."

Then he thought about his best friend. "I sure would like to see Tim McDonald and his wife one more time." As he spoke, his voice broke and he began to cry.

Finally shaking off his emotions, Rawlins stood up straight and asked again about the sheriff. "We've got a little time," a jailer said. "Do you want to make a statement to the people outside?"

Joe went to the window near his cell on the second floor and peered down at the crowd. In a booming voice, much like the preacher he once was, he said: "Gentleman and ladies, white and colored, I want to tell you that I am going in the presence of the almighty Lord. But my boys are innocent of killing the Carter children or having anything to do with it. Me and my boys are as innocent of this crime as you are. My boys never saw Alf Moore until he was brought into this jail. Alf could not even tell them apart. Well, I am going in the presence of a just God and I tell you again my three boys are absolutely innocent of this crime."

A few minutes later, Alf Moore was taken from the cell on the lower floor and brought to the same window to address the crowd. In a strong voice, he said:

> To one and all, this is the man named Alf Moore. I am sorry for the man that got me here, sorry for his children. That man is J.G. Rawlins. And I tell you all, don't let any man lead you into something that is wrong. That is what brought me here. If I had taken the chance to turn away from wrong, I would be out of here now and not almost in the presence of the good Lord. I am sorry from the bottom of my heart for those boys. They were led into it. I asked Mr. Rawlins if it wouldn't be better for him to go with me to do this killing, but he said, 'They will help you and not mind it.' The leader in this killing was Milton Rawlins. I know because I see'd it with my own eyes.
>
> I have told the truth all this time, and I am the happiest man in town. I am going home. I know I have been forgiven, and I am going to heaven. Good-bye to you all. And farewell to the world.

Rawlins listened intently for Moore to exonerate the boys, and when it was not forthcoming, Rawlins muttered, "He's going home, all right." Then he told a guard, "Keep your ears open. You may hear a squeal before they tie that rope around his neck."

Just after eleven o'clock, the doomed men were led to the room where the ominous scaffold towered upward. About twenty-five guards, ministers, physicians and newspaper reporters were crowded into the space in front of the scaffold. Rawlins walked to the platform and sat down on the steps. Moore walked over to him and shook hands with him and said, "Do you realize now that we are going into eternity together?"

Rawlins nodded and then the two men started arguing the case again.

"You gonna tell the truth, Alf?" Rawlins asked.

"I have told the truth, Mr. Rawlins."

"The hell you have. You're a lying...."

The sheriff stepped between them. "It's too late for any of that. Both of you calm down," Passmore said.

Then he turned to two ministers who were present and asked if they wanted to offer a prayer. As each took a turn praying, Moore bowed his head and offered an "Amen!" several times. Rawlins paid no attention to the preachers and chose to look around, mouthing a few silent words to one of the reporters.

The sheriff then led the condemned men to the platform and started to tie their hands. Moore suddenly asked if he might also offer a prayer. When the sheriff nodded assent, Moore knelt at Rawlins' feet, put a hand on Rawlins' knee and prayed, "Oh, Lord, I ask you this morning to have mercy on the soul of J.G. Rawlins."

"Amen!" shouted Rawlins.

"Oh, Lord, this morning I ask you to purge his heart and forgive his sins. I ask you to save his soul before he passes into eternity and it is too late. For Jesus sake, amen!"

Both men were then led onto the trap door.

Moore began singing an old Negro ballad and continued to sing even after a black cap was placed over his head. As the sheriff adjusted the cap, Moore stopped singing long enough to ask for a handkerchief to be tied over his eyes. The sheriff complied.

As the rope was being placed around Rawlins' neck, he smiled nervously and indicated to the sheriff how it should be placed "so it won't choke me too soon."

When all was ready, the sheriff asked each man if he had any last words.

Moore said, "Farewell. If all of you is satisfied and it is the will of the Lord, I am willing to go."

Rawlins said, "I want to say once more that my sons, Milton, Jesse and Leonard, are innocent of this crime. That is all I have to say."

Sheriff Passmore said, "Lord have mercy on your souls," and immediately pulled the rope that released the trap door, sending the men into a fall of seven feet. Rawlins appeared to be dead in an instant, his body hardly twitching. Moore's feet and legs writhed only slightly and then he was still.

A moment after the trap door released, screams could be heard from Lola and Leila who were in the jail but did not witness the execution. They knew the sound of the trap door meant the end of their father's life.

In their cells, Jesse and Leonard cried. Milton, who could be every bit as stoically indifferent in dire circumstances as his father, bit his lip and stared at his hands. If he cried, his tears were few.

Angeline Rawlins, herding her two daughters ahead of her, started across the street to Ulmer's Undertaking Parlor. She was wearing a black hat with a black veil and she had pulled the veil down just before the hanging. But as she started to leave the jail, she decided that she would not give the curious crowd a chance to whisper and wonder if she was crying. She lifted the veil, brushed a strand of hair away from her face and went across the street with her head up and her face expressionless.

Even in the worst of circumstances, the *Atlanta Morning News* noted, Angeline Jowers Rawlins was still "a woman of intense pride, and indeed a woman of rare courage."

There was a stillness about the jail the remainder of the day and through the night. The *Macon Telegraph* called it "the calm after the storm." Jailers spoke mostly in whispers and the usual banter between prisoners had been dampened by the executions.

The Rawlins boys, seemingly in a state of deep depression, asked that visitors other than their mother and sisters not be admitted to the jail. They said they didn't feel like talking to reporters and they didn't want curiosity seekers gawking at them.

Some of the stillness surely could be attributed to the absence of Joe Rawlins. For almost eighteen months, he had talked often and talked loud. His conversations with people through the jailhouse window had become daily fare for hundreds.

Then he was gone. A widow in black was escorting his body to Telfair County for burial at Blockhouse Church cemetery.

As soon as the shock that accompanied the hangings began to wear off, the most-asked question on the street was, "What about the boys?" Cooper announced he would continue the fight to save Milton and Jesse.

As it turned out, he did not encounter much opposition. Two days after their father was hanged, the boys' sentences were commuted to life in prison.

When a *Daily Times* reporter carried the board's decision to the jail, the boys showed little emotion. Even with their father no longer there to shield them and encourage them to follow his line of reasoning, Milton and Jesse maintained that they would rather hang than spend a lifetime in prison. Jesse finally offered a smile and said, "I'd like to see Ma's face when she finds out. I know she will be happy."

If court officials thought a confession might be forthcoming after the hanging, they were disappointed. In fact, the boys seemed to fortify themselves by freely discussing their father's nerve as he went on the gallows.

"Pa was a mighty good man," Milton said, "until he got into this scrape. He always treated us good and half the things said about him just ain't so. I never knew him to lie until he made that confession."

Alf Moore was buried in a Negro cemetery in Valdosta. His grave was never marked.

Joe Rawlins' body arrived in Telfair County on Thursday, and a grieving mother threw herself across the casket and said, "Joey, my Joey, it has been so long for you and for me." And she wept.

A funeral service was held on December 7 in the cemetery at Blockhouse Church. As the casket was being lowered into the grave, a reporter arrived and informed Angeline Rawlins that the death sentences of her two sons had been commuted to life in prison. She smiled.

A marker was placed at Joe Rawlins' grave bearing an epitaph he penned while awaiting execution. It reads:

> *This bark was well built but misguided,*
> *Run swift on the rocks of destruction.*

EPILOGUE

THE RAWLINS FAMILY

Angeline Rawlins—returned to her father's farm near Ambrose, lived in the house her father had built as a wedding present and never remarried. Court records in Coffee County indicate that she dealt extensively in land, buying and selling numerous parcels at a time when the land market was booming. She died November 26, 1931, at age 66. She is buried in the cemetery at New Hope Baptist Church near Ambrose. Her epitaph reads, *Faithful to her Trust even unto Death.*

Milton Rawlins—was sent to the convict camp in Fargo to work in a state-owned lumber mill and later to the Mitchell County convict farm. He was paroled on June 9, 1923, after eighteen years in prison. He returned to Coffee County, married and raised a family. He died on June 26, 1950, at age 64. He also is buried in the cemetery at New Hope Baptist Church near Ambrose.

Leonard Rawlins—was sent to the Babcock convict camp near Bainbridge. He was paroled on November 17, 1911, after spending a little more than five years in prison. He moved to Colorado, married and raised three children there. He returned to Coffee County in the late 1940s. He died on April 17, 1966, two days before his 78th birthday. He also is buried in the cemetery at New Hope Baptist Church near Ambrose.

Jesse Rawlins—was sent to a convict camp at Macon and worked as a steam shovel operator at Cherokee Brick Company, which used a lot of convict labor at the time. He was paroled on Nov. 17, 1911, the same day as his brother, Leonard. He returned to Coffee County, married and raised seven children. He died on August 25, 1939, and is buried in the cemetery at New Hope Baptist Church near Ambrose.

Lola Rawlins Croft—lived in Coffee County, married and raised a family. She died on October 16, 1976, and she is buried in the cemetery at New Hope Baptist Church near Ambrose.

Leila Rawlins—married and moved to Florida. Vital statistics on her could not be found.

THE CARTER FAMILY

William L. Carter—who was born in Macon County, moved to Berrien County in 1906 and returned to Lowndes County in 1918 to sell the 305 acres of land where the killings happened. He and his wife, Ella, raised five sons—Dewitt, Jimmie Lee, David, Lee and Walter—who were in the house the night of the killings, and they became prominent businessmen in Tift, Ware and Lowndes counties. He died on August 21, 1921, a month before his 70th birthday. He is buried in the cemetery at Pine Grove Baptist Church in Berrien County.

Ella Armstrong Carter—who was born in Washington County, moved to Tifton after her husband's death and died on December 2, 1929. She is buried in the cemetery at Pine Grove Baptist Church in Berrien County.

Willie H. and Carrie B. Carter—the two murder victims, are buried in the same grave in the cemetery at Fellowship Baptist Church two miles east of Cecil, Ga., in Cook County.

Lora Carter—died on May 6, 1929, at age 44. She is buried in Tifton.

OTHERS

J.J. "Squire" Jowers—continued to use his money and influence to try to free his grandsons. He died on June 6, 1919, four years before Milton was paroled. However, the fact that the other two brothers, Jesse and Leonard, were released from prison on the same day—November 17, 1911—speaks of either a remarkable coincidence or the influence of a doting grandfather to get them paroled. Jowers is buried in the cemetery at New Hope Baptist Church near Ambrose. This patriarch's place of rest is surrounded by the graves of his wife, children, grandchildren and others close to him.

John Randolph Cooper—went on to become one of Georgia's most prominent attorneys for arguing cases before the U.S. Supreme Court. The *Macon Telegraph* said there was "never a more striking figure in the legal annals of Georgia. His reputation was built on the 'never give up' policy...and he sometimes used his own money to carry on a legal fight. He carried fifteen capital cases to the Supreme Court of the United States."

His dedication was never more apparent than it was in the Rawlins case. He continued his fight for the Rawlins boys until Milton, the last to go free, was released in 1923, eighteen years after the crime and less than a year before Cooper's death. Cooper twice ran for Congress but lost both races.

Born on a farm near Lawrenceville, Ga., in 1865, he proudly claimed to be "a Georgia plowboy" and stayed on the farm until he was 21. He entered the University of Georgia in December 1886 and graduated in July 1890. He set up a law practice in Macon the same year.

Cooper died on April 24, 1924, from a stroke he suffered while on a business trip to Crawford County. He is buried in Lawrenceville.

Solicitor W.E. Thomas—went on to become a Superior Court judge in Lowndes County. On the day Jesse Rawlins appeared in court to hear his sentence commuted to life in prison, Jesse issued a threat to Thomas. "You ain't seen the last of me, Mr. Thomas. I'll be back. You'll see me again. Remember I said that." Sometime after young Rawlins was paroled in 1911, he returned to Valdosta and greeted the judge from the doorway of his office. "Remember me? Jesse Rawlins?" For a moment, the judge later told his daughter, he felt a little apprehensive. But then Jesse stuck out a hand and said, "I came by to thank you. You helped straighten out our lives."